THE ORIGINS OF AMERICA'S JIHADISTS

Brian Michael Jenkins

Perspective
EXPERT INSIGHTS ON A TIMELY POLICY ISSUE

RAND CORPORATION

Contents

Updated December 5, 2017, to correct minor errata.

For more information on this publication, visit www.rand.org/t/PE251.

Summary of Key Judgments

The U.S. homeland faces a multilayered threat from terrorist organizations that could try to carry out a major terrorist operation in the United States or sabotage a U.S.-bound airliner, from Americans returning from jihadist fronts or European returnees who might try to enter the United States, and from homegrown terrorists inspired by jihadist ideology to carry out attacks in the United States. Homegrown jihadists account for most of the terrorist activity in the United States since 9/11.

American Muslims appear unreceptive to the violent ideologies promoted by al Qaeda and the Islamic State of Iraq and Syria (ISIS). A small fraction express favorable views of the tactics that those organizations use, but expressions of support for political violence do not translate to a willingness to engage in violence.

Efforts by jihadist terrorist organizations to inspire terrorist attacks in the United States have thus far yielded meager results. This essay identifies 86 plots to carry out terrorist attacks and 22 actual attacks since 9/11. These involve 178 planners and perpetrators. (This total does not include those who provided material support to jihadist groups or left the United States to join jihadist groups abroad but who did not participate in terrorist attacks or plots to carry out attacks here.)

American jihadists are made in the United States, not imported. Of the 178 jihadist planners and perpetrators, 86 were U.S.-born citizens. The others were naturalized U.S. citizens (46) or legal permanent residents (23)—in other words, people who had long residencies in the United States before arrest. (One more was a U.S. citizen, but it is unclear whether he was born here or naturalized.) Eight of the 178 terrorist attackers and plotters were in the United States on temporary visas, three were asylum seekers, four had been brought into the country illegally (three as small children and one as a teenager), and two were refugees. Three foreigners were participants in a plot to attack John F. Kennedy (JFK) International Airport but did not enter the United States. The status of the remaining few is unknown.

The nation has invested significant resources in preventing terrorist attacks. Public statements indicate that federal and local authorities have followed hundreds of thousands of tips and conducted thousands of investigations since 9/11. An average of 11 people per year have carried out or have been arrested for plotting jihadist terrorist attacks.

Authorities have been able to uncover and thwart most of the terrorist plots, keeping the total death toll under 100 during the 15-year period since 9/11—clearly a needless loss of life but a remarkable intelligence and law enforcement success.

No American jihadist group has emerged to sustain a terrorist campaign. There is no evidence of an active jihadist underground to support a continuing terrorist holy war. There has been no American intifada, just an occasional isolated plot or attack.

Out of tens of millions of foreign arrivals every year, including temporary visitors, immigrants, and refugees, 91 people known to have been born abroad were involved in jihadist terrorist plots since 9/11. Information on arrival dates is available for 66 of these entrants—only 13 of them arrived in the country after 9/11, when entry procedures were tightened. Vetting is not a broken system.

Nationality is a poor predictor of later terrorist activity. Foreign-born jihadists come from 38 countries. Most are Muslim majority (with Pakistan leading the list), but concern about possible attempts by returning European foreign fighters to enter the United States requires looking at a larger set of national origins.

Vetting people coming to the United States, no matter how rigorous, cannot identify those who radicalize here. Most of the foreign jihadists arrived in the United States when they were very young. The average age upon arrival was 14.9 years. The average age at the time of the attack or arrest in a terrorist plot was 27.7. Determining whether a young teenager might, more than 12 years later, turn out to be a jihadist terrorist would require the bureaucratic equivalent of divine foresight.

Of the 25 people involved in actual jihadist terrorist attacks, only one returned to the United States after training abroad with clear intentions to carry out an attack. Adding the "shoe" and "underwear" bombers (bringing the total to 27) makes three entering the country or boarding a U.S.-bound airliner with terrorist intentions. Six others entered or returned to the United States within several years of the attack, but subsequent investigations turned up no proof of connections with terrorist groups while they were abroad. The 18 others (72 percent) had no record of recent travel abroad.

The complexity of terrorist motives defies easy diagnosis. Religious beliefs and jihadist ideologies play an important role but are only one component of a constellation of motives. Remote recruiting has increasingly made jihadist ideology a conveyer of individual discontents. Feelings of alienation, anger, vengeance, disillusion, dissatisfaction, and boredom; life crises; and even mental disabilities appear in the life stories of individual jihadists.

Some of those engaged in jihadist attacks had previously come to the attention of the authorities. Several of these, including the shooter in Little Rock, Arkansas, one of the Boston bombers, and the attacker who killed 49 people in Orlando, Florida, had been interviewed by Federal Bureau of Investigation (FBI) officials at some point in their history and were assessed as posing no immediate danger.

In some cases, that assessment might have been correct at the time, but personal circumstances changed the person's trajectory. Predicting dangerousness is difficult.

The Origins of America's Jihadists

Preventing terrorist attacks on American soil by jihadist extremists remains the paramount objective of U.S. counterterrorist efforts. This essay looks at 178 people who, following instructions from or inspired by the ideologies of jihadist organizations, have carried out or plotted to carry out terrorist attacks in the United States since 9/11. This is not a statistical sample. As of early June 2017, it is the universe of America's jihadist terrorist plotters. (The list of cases and individuals, along with a discussion of the criteria for their inclusion, are provided in the appendix.)

How did these jihadists get here? If they were already here, how did they become jihadists? Whether most of these terrorists come from abroad or are homegrown has policy implications. Concern about terrorist infiltrators calls for tight border controls, travel restrictions, and thorough vetting to keep potential jihadists out. Homegrown terrorism calls for domestic efforts to counter the propagation of extremist ideologies and terrorist recruiting in the community and on the Internet. These topics have become a matter of intense political debate.

This essay reflects continuing research aimed at improving understanding of the nature of the current jihadist terrorist threat to the U.S. homeland. It is intended to assist in efforts to vet visitors, assimilate immigrants and refugees, and better understand who is being locally recruited to terrorist violence.

From Infiltrators to Homegrown Terrorists

Perceptions of the terrorist threat that Islamist extremists pose have evolved over the past quarter-century (see Box 2.1). Throughout the 1990s and during much of the first decade of the 21st century, U.S. authorities viewed jihadist terrorism primarily as an external threat. The 1993 World Trade Center bombing, the subsequent plot to bomb New York City landmarks, and the 1999 plan to detonate a bomb at Los Angeles International Airport were all perceived as being instigated and assisted from abroad, although the earlier cases involved a combination of foreign terrorist operatives and local confederates. The 9/11 attacks clearly were a foreign-directed strategic operation carried out by al Qaeda, whose operatives had infiltrated the United States months earlier.

Fearing that further large-scale attacks might be in preparation or already in the pipeline, the United States

> Out of tens of millions of foreign arrivals every year, including temporary visitors, immigrants, and refugees, 91 people known to have been born abroad were involved in jihadist terrorist plots since 9/11.

Box 1. Foreign-Based Terrorist Plots Against the U.S. Homeland

Since 9/11, jihadist groups have tried to launch attacks on the United States from abroad and inspire homegrown terrorists to carry out attacks in the United States. The latter effort has had a measure of success. None of the attacks from abroad has succeeded.

2001—Shoe bomber. Richard Reid, a United Kingdom (UK)–born jihadist training with al Qaeda in Afghanistan, was equipped with an improvised explosive device that fit in the heel of his shoe. He attempted to blow up a U.S.-bound airliner.

2001—Second shoe bomber. Saajid Badat, a UK-born jihadist, admitted in 2005 that he had also been equipped with a shoe bomb and was supposed to have carried out an attack at the same time as Reid but backed out.

2002—Further hijackings. According to the White House in 2005 and 2006, al Qaeda planned a second hijacking attack to take place in mid-2002. The second attack involved operatives who would breach the cockpit doors using shoe bombs and then crash the plane into the Los Angeles Library Tower (now U.S. Bank Tower). Al Qaeda also planned another hijacking attack to take place on the East Coast to occur in mid-2003.

2003—Plot to disperse cyanide on New York's subways. Little is known about this plot, which involved the planned dispersal of cyanide at several locations in New York's subway system. Reportedly, al Qaeda's second-in-command called it off.

2004—Plot to bomb U.S. financial institutions. Intelligence obtained in Pakistan indicated that Dhiren Barot, an Indian-born jihadist, had proposed to carry out a series of bombings targeting financial institutions, which he had reconnoitered while living in the United States. He was also planning attacks in the UK, where he was arrested and convicted. (Because his plans were formulated while he was a U.S. resident, I include him in our database.)

2006—Plot to detonate a bomb in the Port Authority Trans-Hudson (PATH) train tunnel under the Hudson River. Lebanese authorities arrested Assam Hammoud, a Lebanese jihadist, along with seven others, all non-U.S. persons whom Hammoud recruited to infiltrate the United States and set off backpack bombs on the PATH train between New Jersey and New York.

2006—Plot to sabotage U.S.-bound airliners using liquid explosives. UK police uncovered a plot to smuggle liquid explosives aboard U.S.-bound airliners. Eight people, none from the United States, were ultimately convicted.

2009—Underwear bomber. Umar Abdulmutallab attempted to detonate an explosive device concealed in his underwear aboard a U.S.-bound airliner.

2010—Cargo-plane bomb plot. Foreign intelligence led to the discovery of bombs that had been planted on two U.S.-bound cargo aircraft. Neither device was detonated.

2012—Suicide bomber plot to sabotage a U.S.-bound airliner. A suicide bomber sent by al Qaeda in the Arabian Peninsula to bring down a U.S.-bound airliner was foiled when the operative turned out to be a double agent working for Saudi Arabia.

2017—Possible plot to sabotage U.S.-bound airliners. Details are unavailable, but restrictions imposed on bringing laptops aboard U.S.-bound airliners flying from the Middle East suggest the discovery of new plans to sabotage U.S. airliners.

NOTE: Only four of these plots require infiltrating operatives into the United States. The remaining plots require only that foreign-based terrorists be able to get an operative or a package aboard a U.S.-bound airliner.

promptly initiated a military campaign to destroy al Qaeda's terrorist enterprise in Afghanistan, at the same time casting a broad net to apprehend or kill its operational leaders wherever they could be found, not knowing whether other terrorist operatives might already be inside the United States planning new attacks or laying low while awaiting instructions.

Shortly after the attacks, the U.S. Attorney General directed the FBI and other federal law enforcement personnel to use "every available law enforcement tool" to arrest those who "participate in, or lend support to, terrorist activities." Within two months of the attacks, law enforcement authorities had detained, at least for questioning, more than 1,200 citizens and aliens nationwide. These were persons of interest defined largely on the basis of nationality, religion, and gender—most were Arab and South Asian males who were not U.S. citizens.[1]

> The terrorist plots uncovered in the . . . years [following 9/11] were unconnected, one-off incidents; there was no evidence of a jihadist terrorist underground.

A separate program called the National Security Entry–Exit Registration System mandated that foreigners arriving in the United States from certain Arab and Muslim countries be fingerprinted, photographed, and interviewed. In addition, all males between the ages of 16 and 45 from the designated countries who were already living in the United States and not legal permanent residents or refugees were required to register with federal authorities.[2]

Although theoretically based on tips from the public, the post-9/11 sweeps could be described as preventive detention, driven by profiling, not by evidence of wrongdoing. The actions reflected enormous pressure on authorities to act quickly to prevent another attack when there was little confidence in intelligence, which had so clearly failed on 9/11. In all, about 6,000 people were taken into custody in the months following 9/11. The effort uncovered no new terrorist plots, although it did lead to several arrests on crimes related to terrorism (and sometimes for crimes unrelated to terrorism). According to the Justice Department's own investigation, not one of those detained was ever charged with an act of terrorism. However, five others caught up in the initial sweeps were charged with crimes related to terrorism. One was acquitted, two were convicted on terrorism charges, and the fourth was convicted of visa fraud, although their convictions were later overturned.[3] There was no terrorist plot.

No terrorist networks were uncovered, and none of the individuals registered was convicted of a terrorism-related crime, although many were deported for immigration violations.[4] The terrorist plots uncovered in the following years were unconnected, one-off incidents; there was no evidence of a jihadist terrorist underground.

Nonetheless, the notion of a vast network of jihadist sleeper cells persists.

Some of the attempted attacks and reported threats after 9/11 pointed to a continuing threat from abroad. In December 2001, the so-called shoe bomber attempted to sabotage a U.S.-bound flight. The plan, the bomb, and the bomber were all foreign imports. In 2002, the FBI arrested a U.S. citizen who had earlier joined and trained with al Qaeda and who had been sent back to the United States to carry out a terrorist attack.[5] Authorities reported a 2003 plot to release cyanide in New York's subways but believe that al Qaeda later abandoned the idea.[6] Lebanese authorities uncovered another plot to bomb New York's subway in 2006.[7] A month later, UK authorities uncovered a plot to smuggle liquid explosives aboard U.S.-bound airliners. A further attempt to bring down a U.S. airplane occurred in 2009, when another foreign national recruited abroad tried to detonate an explosive device concealed in his underwear. Two more devices were smuggled aboard U.S.-bound courier aircraft in 2010. These incidents contributed to the conclusion that the continuing jihadist terrorist threat was foreign.

During the same period, however, U.S. authorities began to also uncover local terrorist plots initiated by self-radicalized U.S. residents. These included a 2004 plan to bomb a New York subway station during the Republican National Convention, a 2005 plot to attack targets in Southern California, a 2006 plot to bomb what was then called the Sears Tower in Chicago, and plots in 2007 to attack Fort Dix in New Jersey and JFK International Airport in New York.[8]

As military operations in Afghanistan and arrests of al Qaeda operatives abroad degraded the terrorist organization's ability to launch major international terrorist attacks, homegrown terrorism became the principal concern.[9] The turning point came in 2009 with the arrest of individuals plotting to blow up a synagogue in New York; a shooting attack on an Army recruiting office in Little Rock, Arkansas, that left one person dead and one wounded; a homegrown plot to attack the Marine Corps training base at Quantico, Virginia; a nearly successful plot to carry out suicide bombings in New York's subways; a plot to blow up a federal building in Springfield, Illinois; and the attack by Nidal Hasan at Fort Hood, Texas, which left 13 dead and 32 others injured. Although some of the conspirators had contact with jihadist leaders on the Internet and a few had trained abroad, these were homegrown terrorists.

The Obama administration, which took office in 2009, was determined to adopt a different approach from that of its predecessor by reducing U.S. military operations abroad, although the President reinforced U.S. troops in Afghanistan and escalated the use of drones and special operations to attack al Qaeda leadership.

The Obama administration also showed greater interest in looking for the root causes of terrorism. The return of the phrase *root causes* rankled some old counterterrorism hands who recalled that those opposing U.S. efforts to enlist international cooperation against terrorism in the 1970s and 1980s often used the argument that more needed to be done to examine the root causes of terrorism. Reflecting the so-called national liberation movements and other armed struggles of the era, the suggested causes in the 1970s often included imperialism, colonialism, political oppression, and economic inequality. At the time, this was seen in Western capitals as an oblique effort to justify the use of terrorist tactics when they were employed on behalf of just causes or, at a minimum, as a way of deflecting concerted action until legitimate grievances could be resolved.

Imperialism and colonialism were dropped from the list of root causes in the more recent mentions, but economic and political grievances were still seen as contributing to terrorism. Addressing the White House Summit on Countering Violent Extremism in 2015, President Barack Obama noted that "poverty alone does not cause a person to become a terrorist, any more than poverty alone causes someone to become a criminal. But," he continued, it was necessary to address the grievances that terrorists exploit, including economic grievances:

> [W]hen people—especially young people—feel entirely trapped in impoverished communities, where there is no order and no path for advancement, where there are no educational opportunities, where there are no ways to support families, and no escape from injustice and the humiliations of corruption—that feeds instability and disorder, and makes those communities ripe for extremist recruitment. And we have seen that across the Middle East and we've seen it across North Africa. So if we're serious about countering violent extremism, we have to get serious about confronting these economic grievances.[10]

Some criticized then-President Obama for not identifying "Islamic extremism" as the cause of jihadist terrorism. In fact, he did say that "we have to confront the warped ideologies espoused by terrorists like al Qaeda and ISIL [the Islamic State of Iraq and the Levant, another name for ISIS], especially their attempt to use Islam to justify their violence."

However, the connection between economic grievances and terrorism is more tenuous than the President's remarks suggest. The most economically advanced, liberal democracies, including the United States, have also been the theaters of domestic terrorism campaigns—in many cases, led by the most privileged members of those societies.

The idea of addressing radicalization also gained ground in the years after 9/11. Domestic intelligence efforts depended on understanding how individuals and small groups radicalized. It was learned that the core operatives of the 9/11 operation had been radicalized in Germany before they went to Afghanistan and were enlisted in the 9/11 project. Subsequent terrorist attacks, such as those

The most economically advanced, liberal democracies, including the United States, have also been the theaters of domestic terrorism campaigns—in many cases, led by the most privileged members of those societies.

in Madrid in 2004 and London in 2005, plus the discovery of additional homegrown conspiracies in the United States, offered empirical data for research hypotheses and supported the idea that understanding the trajectory of radicalization could assist in intelligence collection and assessment of the threat posed by people under investigation and provide a basis for programs aimed at countering radicalization. Europe seemed to be ahead of the United States in this area, especially the UK, which, after the 2005 London bombings, initiated efforts to stop people from becoming terrorists or supporting terrorism.[11] By 2011, the UK program was fully operational.

Official U.S. efforts to counter jihadist radicalization began as early as 2007, when members of the U.S. House of Representatives Committee on Homeland Security called for the creation of a National Commission on the Prevention of Violent Extremism and Homegrown Terrorism.[12] The White House outlined a new counter-radicalization approach in an August 2011 strategy paper called *Empowering Local Partners to Prevent Violent Extremism*.[13] However, these early efforts were uncoordinated, and implementation was uneven. Increased recruiting by ISIS gave the program a new sense of urgency, and, in September 2014, the government announced a more focused effort aimed at countering violent extremism (CVE).[14] This more generic term was employed to assure America's Muslim communities that the program was not focused only on Muslims but rather would address all violent extremists. Few were convinced.

CVE was an effort to push even further upstream, albeit with a softer touch, encouraging intervention at the frontier of beliefs. Its basic premise is that people at risk of dangerous thinking can be recognized and discouraged.

Prevention remained the goal. New laws expanding the definition of material support for terrorism and allowing prosecution on the basis of intentions alone gave authorities greater powers to intervene before an attack took place.[15] CVE was an effort to push even further upstream, albeit with a softer touch, encouraging intervention at the frontier of beliefs. Its basic premise is that people at risk of dangerous thinking can be recognized and discouraged. On the one hand, this approach seemed better than prosecuting and jailing those identified as would-be terrorists caught up in police undercover operations. On the other hand, it put authorities in the business of patrolling ideologies, an activity with potentially ominous consequences.

In 2015, the White House convened a three-day summit devoted to CVE; created a senior-level, full-time CVE coordinator in the U.S. Department of Homeland Security (DHS); and announced federally supported pilot projects to take place in three cities.[16] (Despite its high-profile rollout, CVE has yet to become a coherent national effort.) Meanwhile, events in the Middle East again modified perceptions of the terrorist threat.

The Return of the Foreign Threat

The years after the 2011 Arab uprisings saw the rapid escalation of the civil war in Syria, a growing role by jihadist formations in the insurgent movement, a schism in the ranks of al Qaeda, the emergence of ISIS, and its sweep across Iraq and declaration of a so-called caliphate in 2014. This sequence of events brought American attention back to the threat from abroad.

ISIS's initial military successes and its pronouncement of an "Islamic State" galvanized Muslim extremists. Local jihadist movements across North Africa and the Middle East, which had already exploited the chaos and the distraction of authorities that the uprisings caused, declared their support for ISIS. Other jihadist enterprises that had been considered moribund showed signs of new life.

ISIS also used the Internet and social media far more effectively than al Qaeda did to reach a broader audience through a more accessible style of communication. In response, tens of thousands of people from other countries flocked to ISIS, some to live under what they saw as authentic Muslim rule, others to fight. The rebellion and the Assad regime's brutal response had already made Syria a magnet for foreign fighters. By 2016, the U.S. Department of State estimated that as many as 40,000 foreign fighters had traveled to Syria, more than 5,000 of them from Europe.[17] Between 25,000 and 30,000 foreign fighters were reportedly serving in the ranks of ISIS alone. These were far greater numbers than the number of those who traveled to Afghanistan to join the ranks of the mujahid fighting Soviet forces there in the 1980s.

The collapse of Iraq's army and an imminent threat of ISIS massacres of civilian populations in 2014 brought the United States back into the conflict. A U.S.-led air campaign was extended to Syria and included not only ISIS targets but also al Qaeda's Syrian affiliate. By mid-2017, the territory held by ISIS had been significantly reduced, although fighting continued in the Iraqi city of Mosul, and fighting in the ISIS capital, Raqqa, Syria, had only just begun. Military progress raised fears that the defeat of ISIS on the ground would scatter the foreign fighters, who could not survive in a continuing underground contest and would therefore migrate to other fronts or return home, bringing the armed jihad with them.

The past three years have already seen a sharp increase in the number of terrorist attacks in Europe and an uptick in jihadist attacks in the United States, including the 2015 armed assaults in Chattanooga, Tennessee; Garland, Texas; and San Bernardino, California; and the 2016 attacks in Orlando, Florida; St. Cloud, Minnesota; New York and New Jersey; and Columbus, Ohio. None of these attacks involved Americans returning from Syria, although many of them were inspired by ISIS propaganda. They brought fear levels back to where they had been in the months immediately after 9/11.[18]

Many people in the United States perceived the events in Europe to be a consequence of uncontrolled immigration, exacerbated by the massive influx of refugees from the Middle East and "politically correct" multicultural domestic policies that threatened social cohesion and impeded a vigorous response. American critics pointed to Europe's inadequate border controls and uncoordinated intelligence efforts, which enabled terrorist infiltrators and returning fighters to come back undetected and link up with locals to carry out spectacular attacks, such as those in Paris in November 2015 and Brussels in March 2016. U.S. officials also worried that European jihadists would be able to exploit the Visa Waiver Program and get into the United States.

Donald Trump's new presidential administration portrayed the terrorist threat as coming from abroad, to be met by restricting the flow of refugees, immigrants, and visitors to the United States until more-rigorous vetting measures could be put into place. The attacks in Europe were presented as what could happen in the United States if barriers—both physical and procedural—were not erected. Whether or not this was an accurate portrayal of the terrorist threat, as a political message, it played well among Americans who were already anxious about immigration, especially illegal immigration; refugees from conflict zones; and changing ethnic demographics; as well as general economic malaise.

> Homegrown terrorists account for most of the terrorist attacks and plots in the United States since 9/11. This continues to be the most likely type of incident.

A Multilayered Threat

As the discussion above indicates, the United States currently confronts a complex, multilayered terrorist threat. Terrorist organizations abroad could make a strategic decision to launch a major terrorist operation against the United States, assembling and training the recruits and facilitating their infiltration with stolen documents or through other means. This would be an operation like that of 9/11 or, more recently, the 2008 terrorist attack on Mumbai. It is not clear that ISIS has made such a decision. And improved intelligence since 9/11 has made this far more difficult, although not impossible. Continuing military pressure on ISIS in Syria and Iraq, as well as on al Qaeda's affiliates, is intended to prevent such an event.

Former Secretary of Homeland Security John F. Kelly indicated recently that he worried about terrorist sabotage of a U.S. or U.S.-bound airliner.[19] There have been several sabotage attempts since 9/11. Authorities have uncovered and thwarted multiple plots, and sabotage remains a real threat. This is not to say that air travel is unsafe. It is DHS's responsibility to prevent even a single event. With tens of thousands of daily flights in or to the United States, the government's task is enormous, but the statistical risk to the individual passenger is negligible.

Returning foreign fighters—Americans or other Western recruits who have served with ISIS, Jabhat Fateh al-Sham (al Qaeda's former affiliate in Syria), or other jihadist fronts in Yemen, Somalia, or elsewhere—pose another layer of threat. One returning veteran of al Qaeda's affiliate in Syria planned to carry out attacks after his return. Intercepting the returnees is a high-priority concern of U.S. authorities.

Despite the possibility of terrorist attacks on the United States from abroad, sabotage of U.S.-bound airliners, or terrorist actions by returning foreign fighters, what al Qaeda and, more successfully, ISIS have done most effectively is inspire some followers already in the United States to take action themselves. Homegrown terrorists account for most of the terrorist attacks and plots in the United States since 9/11 (see Table 1). This continues to be the most likely type of incident. These are low-tech attacks, but they can still be lethal—the 2016 armed assault in Orlando, Florida, was (at the time) the deadliest mass shooting in U.S. history.

The Historical Evidence

The origins of America's jihadists have been addressed in my previous RAND publications, congressional testimony, and published commentary. This continuing research divides people involved in jihadist-inspired terrorist crimes since 9/11 into three broad categories: (1) those who have been arrested in the United States for providing material support to jihadist terrorist organizations—including financial support, weapons, targeting information, recruiting, training, or assisting in disseminating terrorist propaganda; (2) those who have gone abroad to join terrorist fronts or have attempted to do so (the law considers this a form of material assistance, but it

Table 1. Homegrown Terrorist Attacks and Plots Since 9/11

YEAR	ATTACKS	PLOTS
2001	0	0
2002	1	2
2003	0	7
2004	0	5
2005	0	4
2006	1	4
2007	0	2
2008	0	1
2009	2	7
2010	1	6
2011	1	8
2012	0	4
2013	1	4
2014	3	1
2015	4	19
2016	5	11
2017	1	1
TOTAL	20	86

NOTE: A *plot* is a plan to carry out an attack. Some were very specific; others vague. A plan to bomb a target is a plot, even if undercover agents provided a fake explosive that the subject "detonated." *Attack* means an actual attempt, not under control of the authorities, whether or not it succeeded. These figures exclude the attacks by the 2001 shoe bomber, a UK national, and the 2009 underwear bomber, a Nigerian national, on in-bound U.S. airliners, as both were recruited and equipped with bombs abroad and had no nexus with domestic operatives or confederates.

is different in that the person is volunteering to engage in violence); and (3) those who have been arrested for carrying out terrorist attacks or plotting to carry out terrorist attacks in the United States (including those killed during attacks). These three categories reflect different levels of commitment, risk to the perpetrators, and danger to the community. The third category—those who carried out or plotted terrorist attacks here—is the subject of this inquiry.

Some caveats are in order. The numbers of American jihadists in all three categories are very small, limiting confidence in any statistics. Moreover, the numbers are malleable. There is no agreed-upon chronology of cases or single publicly available comprehensive database of jihadist terrorists. In addition, the data are often incomplete. Biographical details about those arrested have to be gleaned from a variety of sources.

The term *plots*, as used here, refers to intentions to carry out attacks in the United States, but some reports apply the term more broadly to include any jihadist-related conspiracy, including those involving only material support, thereby claiming that hundreds of plots have been uncovered. To avoid being accused of omission, this chronology of cases tends toward inclusiveness; even so, there have been fewer than 100 jihadist terrorist plots in the United States since 9/11. (A chronology of the attacks and plots and a list of the 178 people involved are presented in the appendix of this essay.)

No list of jihadist plots or attacks in the United States will satisfy every reader. Some will criticize the omissions; others will say that the inclusions are too broad. Opinions differ on whether some of the attacks that have occurred were motivated by jihadist ideology or by other factors. The legal difference between terrorism and a hate crime can sometimes be blurry. Debate continues about whether the mass shooting at Fort Hood should be classified as terrorism or workplace violence.[20] (Nidal Hasan, the shooter and an Army major, was convicted under the Uniform Code of Military Justice of 13 counts of premeditated murder and 31 counts of attempted murder.) In some cases—notably, the 2017 Fort Lauderdale–Hollywood International Airport shooting—the perpetrator appeared to be mentally ill.[21] Not every street thug or mentally disordered person who happens to be Muslim should be categorized as a terrorist. In any case, the inclusion or omission of a few cases does not appear to significantly alter the conclusions, although further inclusions appear to increase the proportion of U.S.-born citizens.

It must be recognized that these are inherently sensitive topics on which opinions have become increasingly polarized along political lines. Any analysis inevitably touches upon issues of religion, race, and ethnicity. Research must tread carefully through a minefield of animus, agendas, and competing narratives. The solution offered here is that of transparency. The list of attacks and plots and a full list of the people involved are presented in the appendix.

A final caveat: The evidence presented here is historical. It covers a period of more than 16 years—more than four times the length of America's participation in World War II. That, however, is no guarantee that the pattern of jihadist terrorism will not change in the future, requiring commensurate changes in counterterrorist policies and security measures. Terrorist attacks on American soil might dramatically increase in volume or escalate in lethality. Former Secretary of Homeland Security Kelly warned that the threat of a terrorist attack on the United States by foreign fighters returning from Syria or homegrown terrorists "is as threatening today as it was that September morning almost 16 years ago."[22] Others have recently suggested that tomorrow's terrorists might turn to weapons of mass destruction, as so many feared in the shadow of 9/11.

Needles and Haystacks

The U.S. Muslim population is estimated to be about 3.3 million.[23] It consists of both native-born Muslims, many of whom are the descendants of African slaves brought to America between the 17th and 19th centuries, and a more recent population of immigrants who began to arrive from the Middle East in large numbers in the late 1940s. The U.S.-born jihadists come from both of these communities.

Foreign-born terrorists can enter the country as immigrants, as refugees, or on various types of visas. More than 14 million immigrants entered the United States between 2002 and 2016 (see Figure 2).[24] Those coming from Muslim-majority countries accounted for an estimated 18 percent of the 617,752 immigrant visas issued in 2016.[25] In addition, a total of 783,330 refugees entered the United States between 2002 and 2015, 279,339 of whom were recorded as Muslims.[26]

Apart from immigrants and refugees, 380 million people entered the United States on various nonimmigrant visas between fiscal years 2002 and 2015—an average of about 27 million a year. (This excludes the millions of people annually entering on border-crossing cards that are used

Figure 1. Jihadist Threat Is Like a Needle in a Haystack

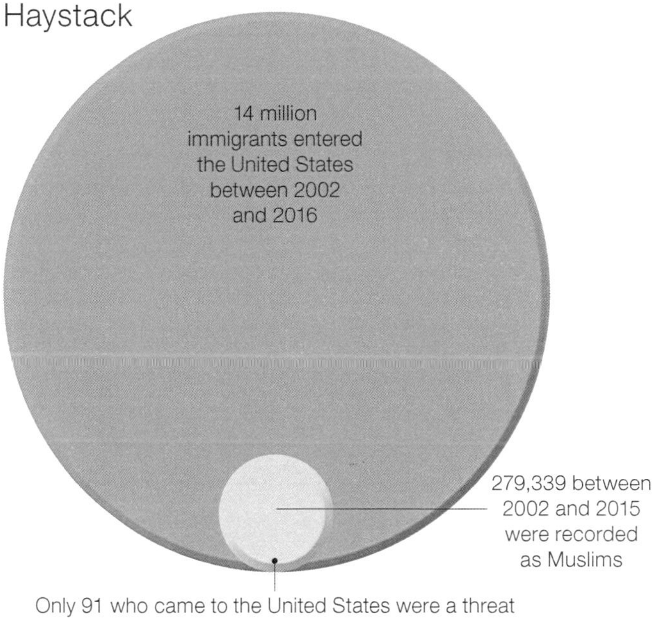

NOTE: The haystack is huge, and there are few jihadis. More than 14 million immigrants entered the United States between 2002 and 2016. In addition, a total of 783,330 refugees entered the United States between 2002 and 2015, 279,339 of whom were recorded as Muslims. Only 91 who came to the United States during this time were a threat.

to go back and forth across the borders with Canada and Mexico and those entering through the Visa Waiver Program.[27]) This volume has been increasing—in the five years from 2011 to 2015, the annual average number of nonimmigrant visas reached 43 million. In 2015 alone, roughly 3 million of the 54 million nonimmigrant visa entries came from the same countries of origin as the foreign-born jihadist plotters identified since 9/11.[28] About four-fifths of the jihadist plotters came from Muslim-majority countries, including Afghanistan, Albania,

Algeria, Bangladesh, Bosnia, Egypt, Iran, Iraq, Jordan, Kashmir, Kosovo, Kuwait, Kyrgyzstan, Lebanon, Morocco, Pakistan, Palestine, Saudi Arabia, Sierra Leone, Somalia, Turkey, Uzbekistan, and Yemen.

Since entries under the Visa Waiver Program began in 1988, it has accounted for more than 300 million entries—more than 200 million between 2002 and 2015.[29] This volume also has been increasing and now averages more than 20 million a year. Brunei is the only Muslim-majority country currently included in the Visa Waiver Program; however, U.S. officials have expressed concern that European jihadists returning from Syria, as European nationals, theoretically would be eligible to enter the United States under the program. Intercepting them would depend on the effectiveness of U.S. intelligence and joint efforts with the European services.

These numbers tell a story. The haystacks are huge, and there are few jihadis. Either foreign jihadist organizations are not trying hard to get in or U.S. screening measures seem to be working. The so-called lone-wolf terrorists appear to be a domestic production, not a border problem. And whether they are born here or abroad, most are arrested before they act.

In the 15.5 years between October 2001 and March 2017, a total of 178 people were arrested or killed in the United States for carrying out or plotting jihadist terrorist attacks (see Figure 2). (This total does not include the shoe bomber and the underwear bomber who boarded U.S.-bound airliners.) This is a very small number.

In addition, more than 100 others (an estimate based on previous research[30]) were arrested for providing material

Figure 2. Origins of America's Jihadists

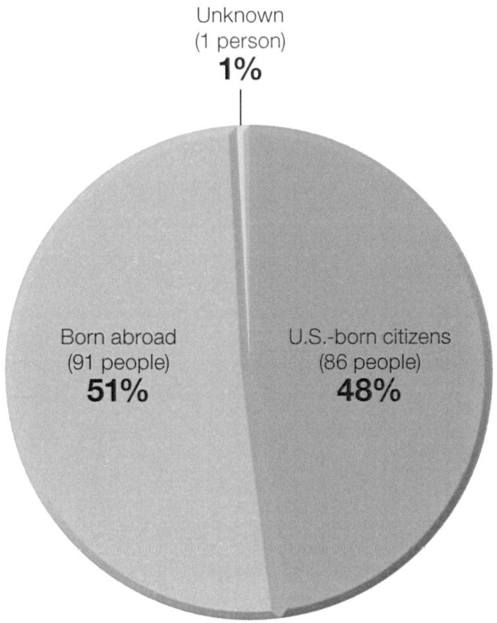

NOTE: In the 15.5 years between October 2001 and March 2017, a total of 178 people were arrested or killed in the United States for carrying out or plotting jihadist terrorist attacks. Of the total of 25 jihadists who were involved in actual terrorist attacks, 14 were born in the United States. If we add to these attackers those who were involved in terrorist plots that were uncovered, a total of 86 were born in the United States and 91 came from abroad. (Information on one person is lacking.)

support to jihadist terrorist organizations, and several hundred more joined or tried to join jihadist groups abroad—there is uncertainty about how many traveled to Syria. Depending on how these are counted, this comes to a combined total of somewhere around 600 for all three categories.

If we confine our inquiry to those carrying out or plotting terrorist attacks in the United States, that works out to approximately ten or 11 terrorist plotters per year, or about one-third of a terrorist plotter for each 100,000 Muslims. Of the total of 25 jihadists who were involved in actual terrorist attacks, 14 were born in the United States. If we add to these attackers those who were involved in terrorist plots that were uncovered, a total of 86 were born in the United States and 91 came from abroad. (Information on one person is lacking.)

How did those who came from abroad get here? Two who were subsequently involved in terrorist plotting arrived as refugees. Others arrived as immigrants or on various temporary visas. Two more, both of whom arrived before 9/11, entered the United States under the terms of the Visa Waiver Program.[31] The first one was arrested upon arrival at the airport in 1992.[32] The second was Zacarias Moussaoui, whose enrollment in a flight training school aroused the suspicion of the FBI, which arrested and held him on visa-violation charges a month before 9/11.[33] Richard Reid, the shoe bomber, also obtained a visa through the Visa Waiver Program, which enabled him to board a U.S.-bound flight in December 2001.[34] In sum, three of the more than 300 million entrants under the Visa Waiver Program in the entire history of the program turned out to be terrorists. Since the shoe bomber, no terrorists have been known to enter the country under the program.

Complete information is available for only 66 of the 91 entrants from abroad who became terrorist plotters after 9/11. Of these, only 13 arrived in the country after 9/11. Overall, those in charge of vetting entrants are looking at ratios between future jihadists and the corresponding populations of foreign arrivals of from less than one per 100,000 to less than one per 100 million. The point here is that only a tiny fraction of those who enter the country as temporary visitors, permanent immigrants, or refugees have subsequently turned out to be terrorists.

Is vetting supposed to prevent terrorists from getting into the United States or to prevent the entry of someone who could one day become a terrorist? If it is the former, the small number suggests that vetting procedures, especially the more rigorous scrutiny imposed after 9/11, have largely worked. Although we do not know how many tried, almost no jihadist terrorist infiltrators are getting in.

Alternatively, the time gap between arrival and involvement in terrorism suggests that the decision to become a terrorist is being made after arrival—foreign-born jihadists are radicalizing here. Whether any sort of vetting can identify and prevent the entry of someone who is not concealing terrorist intentions when they are vetted but who might one day turn into a terrorist is a different question. In other words, can screening pick out future terrorists? That requires knowing more about who becomes a terrorist and why.

Radicalization in the American Muslim Community

The small number of jihadist terrorists identified in the United States would seem to suggest that American Muslims are unreceptive to the violent ideologies promoted by al Qaeda or ISIS. According to Pew Research Center public opinion surveys in 2007 and 2011 (prior to the emergence of ISIS), 5 percent of American Muslims held favorable attitudes toward the violent jihadists.[35] Based on an estimated population of 3.3 million, this

The biographies of those who carry out attacks suggest an irregular course rather than a one-way trajectory leading from increasingly radical views to violent action. Only a tiny percentage of those holding extreme views become violent.

would work out to about 165,000 people, or about 60,000 to 65,000 men. According to the polls, 7 percent of the Muslims in the United States thought that suicide bombings and other terrorist tactics were sometimes justified. One percent thought such tactics were often justified.[36]

This is a smaller percentage than those seen in European countries. According to the Pew Research Center, 10 percent of the Muslims living in France and Spain thought that suicide bombings and other attacks on civilian targets were sometimes justified, while 6 percent thought that such tactics were often justified. In the UK, 12 percent thought that such terrorist tactics were sometimes justified, while 3 percent thought that they were often justified.[37] According to an ICM Unlimited poll conducted one year after 2005 the terrorist bombings, which killed 52 people in London, 20 percent of UK Muslims said they felt some sympathy for the bombers, although 99 percent thought that it was wrong to carry out the attack.[38] In another poll, conducted in 2006 by GfK NOP Social Research, 22 percent of UK Muslims strongly agreed or tended to agree that the terrorist bombings were justified.[39]

This narrower shelf of support for violent extremism in the United States still worried some Muslims and more non-Muslims. Six percent of American Muslims thought there was "a great deal of support for extremism" in the Muslim American community; 15 percent of the general public thought so.[40]

Younger Muslims in the United States might hold more-extreme views than their elders. The 2007 Pew survey found that people under 30 years of age were more than twice as likely as older people to believe that terrorist tactics were justified, although one has to wonder whether publicly expressing such a view in a public survey just six years after 9/11 might reflect some degree of youthful belligerence.[41]

Nine percent of U.S.-born black American Muslims expressed a favorable view of al Qaeda, while 36 percent expressed a very unfavorable view; 56 percent of all American Muslims expressed a very negative view.[42] Black Americans comprise about 59 percent of the converts to Islam in the United States.[43] Jihadist organizations tried to exploit the anger caused by police shootings of black Americans to raise tensions and recruit followers, with little apparent success, although some black American Muslims are among the jihadists.

Observers can debate whether these findings indicate a reservoir of terrorist recruits and sympathizers. Or could there be a small percentage of people holding extreme views on almost any question asked? Caution is in order. Previous RAND research has noted that

> polls designed to measure the extent of support for political violence, or lack thereof, will not accurately reflect radicalization or a willingness to engage in violence. . . . Future studies on radicalization or rejecting extremism should be careful not to equate measures of support for political violence with a willingness to engage in violence.[44]

This observation is critical. Telling pollsters that violence is sometimes or even often acceptable and being willing to engage in violence are separate decisions. One is not the extension of the other. I would go further: Terrorism is, by definition, violence intended to impose one's political views on others. Terrorist tactics are usually employed by extremists seeking fundamental or radical change in the order of things. But not all terrorists come from the ranks of identified radicals.

Of course, American jihadists, by their actions and claimed motives, can be presumed to hold favorable attitudes toward jihadist organizations and approve of terrorist actions, but this does not tell us how important ideology is as a component of their motivations. I cannot say that increasingly radical views alone propel believers to terrorist action. The biographies of those who carry out attacks suggest an irregular course rather than a one-way trajectory leading from increasingly radical views to violent action. Only a tiny percentage of those holding extreme views become violent. We also have seen people following what appears to be a path toward violence veer off only to later return to such a path as a result of changing individual circumstances.

Ideologues might see terrorist violence as an effective means to advance their cause, but, once terrorist organizations take the field, the campaign attracts recruits who are drawn more to the attributes of the armed struggle—participation in a cause, the prestige of membership, the camaraderie of clandestinity, the opportunities for violence. Ideological commitment might be just one, and not necessarily the most important, attraction. As a terrorist campaign continues, it also inevitably attracts criminal types and sociopaths, for whom devotion to an ideology is of even less importance. This phenomenon appears in most terrorist campaigns, not only those of al Qaeda and ISIS.

The difference in contemporary jihadist terrorist recruitment is the Internet. Followers are remotely recruited to action without first joining any group. No one evaluates their political convictions. They are not being admitted to a clandestine organization. There is little concern about their reliability. They are invited to travel to Syria to join a group waging war in the field. Those with little to offer will be cannon fodder. Those who cannot make it to a jihadist front are exhorted to take whatever action they can wherever they are, and those who do so are embraced and applauded—their "membership" comes after the act, not before. Their ideological credentials are irrelevant. They must be fervent in action, not necessarily fervent in belief.

ISIS, an especially bloodthirsty organization, has advertised its atrocities as a means of terrorizing its foes and as proof of its own authenticity. And through social media, it has been able to disseminate appeals and images that are disturbing to most people but resonate with a few. Those willing to take action are self-selectors. Their decisions reflect a combination of ideological motivations and personal, often emotional, factors. The incentives are highly idiosyncratic. For some, religious beliefs or jihadist ideology are a critical component. For others, joining the armed jihad is no more than a vehicle for acting out their anger and aggression.

The difficulty in sorting out the sequence of motives is reflected in the case of Justin Sullivan, a 20-year old U.S.-born convert to Islam and self-proclaimed supporter of ISIS, arrested in 2015 for plotting to carry out mass killings in Virginia and North Carolina. While plotting his terrorist campaign, he told an FBI undercover agent that he also planned to have his parents killed. By then, he had murdered an elderly disabled neighbor as training run. Most media accounts report that Sullivan converted to Islam and began downloading ISIS videos, but, after his arrest, Sullivan recalled that he began watching videos of Islamic State (IS) beheadings and other atrocities in 2014 prior to his conversion. He said "I liked IS from the beginning, then I started thinking about death and stuff so I became a Muslim."[45] This would suggest that it was not Islam but a predisposition toward violence that drove Sullivan to plan a terrorist campaign.

Holding radical views is not a crime in the United States. People have all sorts of ideas about the need for radical change in America and are free to promote their causes. Government interest in radicalization can be justified only when the radicalization leads to violence or material support for violence, which are crimes. Without the presumption of a violent end point, radicalization is off-limits to government action. U.S. officials, therefore, generally speak about "radicalization and recruitment to terrorism" as a single, connected activity, with one leading to the other.

People look for a rational explanation for terrorist savagery. Terrorist violence is random, which is disturbing enough—surely, violence must have a cause. Somehow that makes it less upsetting. But presuming a causal link can be misleading. Radical views and terrorist action overlap, but radicalism and violent radicalism are different domains. When the opportunity arises, however, some percentage of those who hold radical ideas will join in violence.

Radical views and terrorist action overlap, but radicalism and violent radicalism are different domains. When the opportunity arises, however, some percentage of those who hold radical ideas will join in violence.

The goals of differing agendas of the terrorists' foes also come into play. Some strategies view counterradicalization as a means of preventing terrorism, but some influencers have expressed concerns about the broader social problems created by adherence to radical views, whether or not these lead to violence. Terrorism, in this context, is merely one manifestation of a more fundamental problem (i.e., whether a liberal democratic state that adheres to certain core values can successfully assimilate those who are determined to reject its basic principles). And finally, some agendas reflect a more extreme view that Judeo-Christian civilization is inescapably locked in a religious war with Islam—a mirror image of the jihadists' worldview.

Jihadist Marketing Is Producing a Low Turnout

The efforts by both al Qaeda and ISIS to recruit followers and inspire terrorist attacks in the United States have thus far continued to yield meager results, although there was a sharp rise in activity in 2015 and 2016. Since 9/11, there have been 20 jihadist terrorist attacks in the United States. This total excludes the 2001 attempt by the shoe bomber and the 2009 attempt by the underwear bomber to sabotage U.S.-bound airliners. It also excludes several cases in which there was little evidence of a connection to jihadist ideology. The 20 attacks resulted in a total of 95 deaths, not counting the perpetrators who were killed.

In addition, authorities also reportedly uncovered 86 jihadist terrorist plots in the United States.[46] Again, the list of cases presented in the appendix is inclusive. It is not clear that all of these plots would have led to attacks if authorities had not intervened—in several cases, the plots appear to have been fantasies that the perpetrator had little capability to carry out. Neither is it clear whether mental instability or jihadist beliefs were the primary motive. I offer no evaluation of the abilities of those arrested to actually carry out their schemes. A court found them guilty. I offer no assessment of whether justice was done in every case.

In 2017, former Homeland Security Secretary Kelly stated that, since 2013, there have been 37 ISIS-linked plots to attack the United States.[47] It is not clear exactly what is included in this figure. Our chronology includes 14 actual attacks and 36 domestic jihadist plots since 2013.

The United States has suffered no sustained terrorist campaign. Unlike the 1970s, recent years have seen no American jihadist group emerge. There is no evidence of an active jihadist underground to support a continuing terrorist holy war. There has been no American intifada, just an occasional isolated plot and no more than 20 locally initiated attacks since 9/11. There is little evidence of connectivity. Seventeen of the 20 attacks and 59 of the 86 plots involved a single person (although often conspiring with a confidential informant or undercover agent whom that person believed to be a terrorist operative). That means that 72 percent of the 106 cases (plots and attacks) involved one person.

Why has there not been more jihadist terrorism in the United States? Several possibilities come to mind.

America's relentless campaign against al Qaeda reduced the organization's ability to mount attacks from abroad. Attacking the United States does not appear to have had

> It is not measurable statistically, but anecdotal evidence suggests that many in America's Muslim community are not simply deaf to jihadist calls to action—they have discouraged tendencies toward terrorism.

the same strategic priority for ISIS, although it too has been the target of U.S. military operations.

Both al Qaeda and ISIS have attempted to recruit followers in the United States and exhort them to take action, but doing so remotely is difficult, especially when taking action is likely to end in death or long imprisonment.

America's Muslims, except for a very few, appear unreceptive to jihadist ideologies. Most American Muslims are not marginalized or politically disenfranchised, although recent terrorist attacks have created tensions and apprehension. It is not measurable statistically, but anecdotal evidence suggests that many in America's Muslim community are not simply deaf to jihadist calls to action—they have discouraged tendencies toward terrorism. It also could be that those in the best position to recognize tendencies toward extremism among family and friends are intervening in ways not visible to the authorities to dissuade would-be terrorists from a self-destructive path that would subject the entire community to suspicion. The Muslim community has, in fact, been a source of tips to the authorities.

U.S. authorities also have proved to be effective in identifying and arresting would-be terrorists: The conviction rate has been high, and the courts have imposed severe sentences. This has prevented attacks and also could act as a deterrent to all but the most fanatical followers or those least capable of assessing risk.

A Statistical Profile of America's Jihadist Terrorist Plotters

Although the total number of terrorist plotters is small, a group portrait does emerge. The average age of jihadist terrorists at the time of their attack or arrest is 29.2 years (the median is 27). However, jihadist activity appears to be starting at younger ages. Between 2002 and 2008, the average age of American jihadists was 32.2 (the median was 27), whereas, between 2009 and 2017, the average age was 27.5 (the median was 26). The numbers are small, suggesting caution about any statistical inferences, but the trend toward younger recruits could reflect the terrorist organizations' greater reliance on social media, which reaches a younger audience.

At least 48 percent of the American jihadists for whom we know the place of birth were born in the United States (86 people) (see Figures 3 and 4). Others came to the United States from 38 countries: Pakistan, with 18, heads the countries of origin, followed by Somalia (six);

Box 2. Comparing Jihadist Attacks in Europe with Those in the United States Since 9/11

Owing to differences in the law, policing methods, and counting procedures, it is difficult to compare the number of interrupted terrorist plots in Europe with the 83 terrorist plots in the United States; however, it is possible to make some rough comparisons of the actual attacks.

Twenty jihadist attacks in the United States resulted in 95 fatalities (an average of five fatalities per attack). More than half of these fatalities resulted from the 2016 Orlando nightclub attack, in which 49 people died. Putting this outlier aside, the average drops to 2.4 fatalities per attack.

During the same period, jihadists in Europe carried out at least 38 terrorist attacks. These resulted in 492 fatalities (an average of 13 fatalities per attack). However, a single attack in Spain accounts for 191 of the total. If we set this statistical outlier aside, the average number of fatalities per attack drops to eight fatalities per incident.

Four countries (France, the UK, Germany, and Belgium) account for a major portion of the violence, suffering 92 percent of the attacks and 60 percent of the fatalities. The same four countries also provided the greatest number of fighters traveling to Syria to join ISIS, an indicator of radicalization.

The combined population of these four countries is approximately 225 million, or about 70 percent of that of the United States. If Europe's deaths from jihadist terrorism were to be scaled up to the U.S. population, the total number of deaths in America would be around 700, more than seven times the actual total. The impact on U.S. attitudes and policies would be enormous.

The comparison suggests that, as a group, these four European countries have experienced higher levels of radicalization, higher numbers of terrorist attacks with higher levels of lethality, and higher numbers of total fatalities. Although the United States fares far better in the comparison, the apprehension created by the attacks in Europe adds to the overall level of fear in the United States.

Afghanistan (six); Albania, Bangladesh, Guyana, Iraq, Jordan, Morocco, and Saudi Arabia (all with three each); and Uzbekistan (two). Most American jihadists are from Muslim-majority countries, but 11 known jihadists are from Latin America.

Earlier RAND research did not show a significant difference in level of education between American jihadists and other Americans from the same age group. Where information was available, jihadists included roughly the same proportion of school dropouts, high school graduates, and those with some college, university, and postgraduate degrees. A few dropped out of college to become jihadists.[48]

Complete and accurate statistics are not available, but America's jihadists come from diverse socioeconomic backgrounds that appear to differ little from those of the general population. Although there might be a somewhat higher percentage in the lower economic registers, it does not appear that radicalization is a product of poverty or deprivation.

Hardly surprising is the finding that almost all of the jihadist plotters were known to be Muslims; a few might be non-Muslim mercenaries. Estimates of the proportion of jihadists who are converts to Islam run as high as 35 to 40 percent.[49] Our data show that at least 38 percent were converts (although we lack information on eight

Figure 3. The Majority of People Involved in Actual Jihadist Attacks Were from the United States

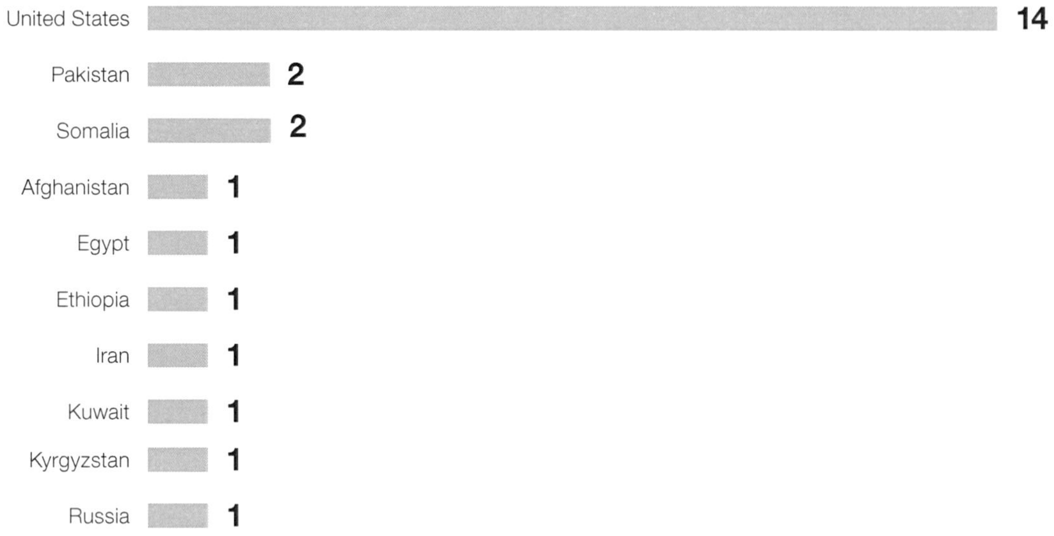

NOTE: A majority of the jihadist attackers were born in the United States. Not counting the shoe bomber and the underwear bomber, 14 of the 25 people who carried out the other 20 jihadist terrorist attacks since 9/11 were born in the United States, seven were naturalized U.S. citizens, three were legal permanent residents, and one was an asylum seeker.

people). About 23 percent of America's Muslims describe themselves as converts to Islam.[50] Islam is a rapidly growing religion, and the proportion of converts could also be increasing.

A higher percentage of converts among the jihadists could reflect life crises. These jihadists might have reached out to a new religion to solve other problems in their lives. Violent behavior could reflect the same personal problems. It could also reflect converts' tendency to become true believers determined to demonstrate their newfound convictions to others and themselves.

Most Jihadists in the United States Are Made in the United States, Not Imported

Not counting the shoe bomber and the underwear bomber—both foreign nationals who were recruited and equipped abroad—14 of the 25 people who carried out the other 20 jihadist terrorist attacks since 9/11 were born in the United States, seven were naturalized U.S. citizens, three were legal permanent residents, and one was an asylum seeker. Of the larger population of 178 jihadists arrested for terrorist attacks and plots, 86 were born in the United States and 46 were naturalized U.S. citizens. Another one was a U.S. citizen, but it is not clear whether

Figure 4. The Majority of Attackers and Plotters Were from the United States

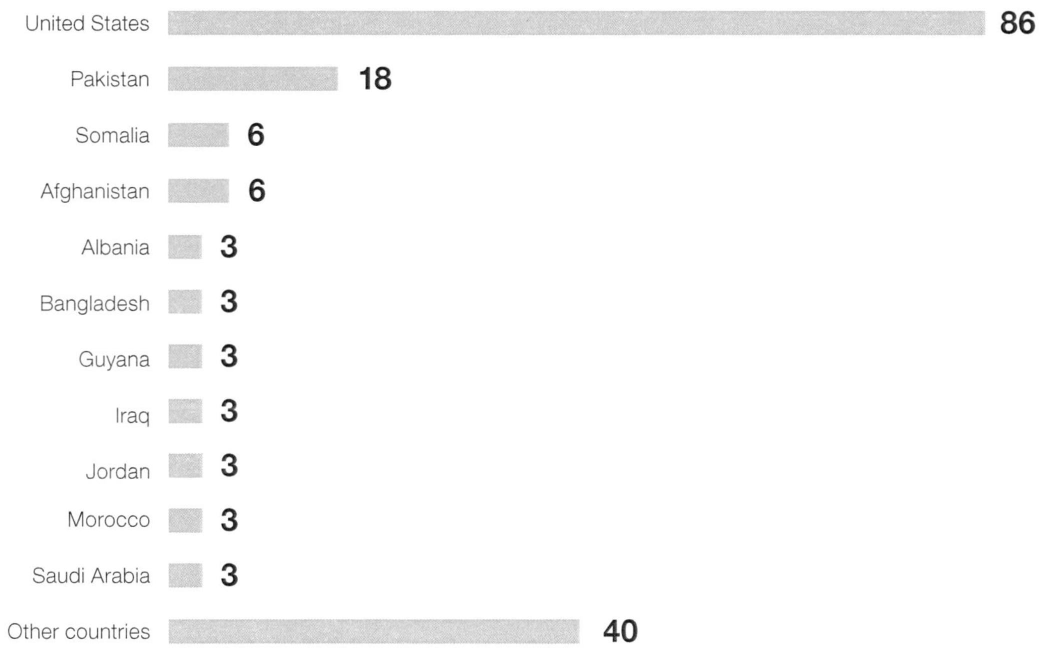

NOTE: U.S.-born citizens account for nearly half of all of the jihadist attackers and plotters, followed by immigrants from Pakistan.

he was born in the United States or naturalized. The remaining 43 were legal permanent residents or in the United States with some other status. (Again, we lack information on the statuses of two people.)

Looking at it another way, we could say that 91 of the 178 were definitely foreign-born, and the birthplace of one is unknown (see Figure 5). Of the foreign-born, 46 (52 percent) became U.S. citizens—an indication of assimilation that is about the same as or somewhat higher than the percentage of all immigrants who become U.S. citizens.[51]

Twenty-three of the 91 foreign-born jihadists were in the United States as legal permanent residents, eight were on some type of temporary visa, three were asylum seekers, two were refugees, and four had entered the country illegally (three as small children with their parents and one as a teenager). Three of the four plotters who were part of the 2007 conspiracy to bomb JFK International Airport never

Figure 5. Status of 91 Foreign-Born Jihadists

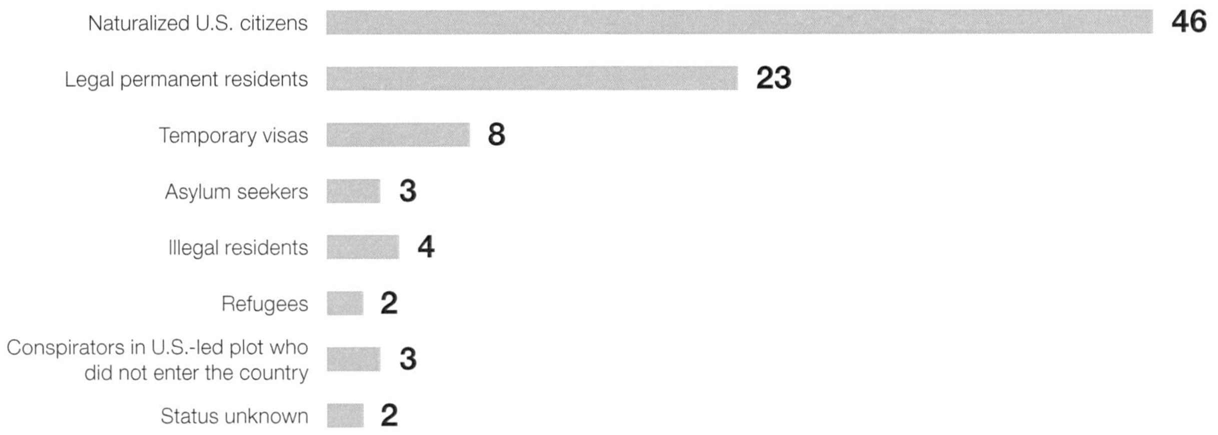

came to the United States.[52] The status of the remaining plotters is unknown. It is not surprising that all but nine of the foreign-born plotters came from Muslim-majority countries. However, that also means that 10 percent of the foreign-born jihadists came from such countries as the UK, France, China, South Korea, Haiti, Cuba, Nicaragua, and the Dominican Republic. In the appendix, we include details about all 178 people.

Entry information is available for 66 of the 91 foreign-born people who came to the United States and subsequently participated in jihadist terrorist attacks or plots. Fifty-one of them were long-time residents who arrived before 9/11. Only 13 arrived in the United States after the 9/11 attacks, which prompted greater scrutiny of all entrants. See the appendix for more information about all 178 people.

Opportunities for vetting arrivals at ports of entry will be limited. Of the 25 people convicted of carrying out jihadist terrorist attacks in the United States, only one arrived or returned to the United States with clear intentions to carry out a terrorist attack. Faisal Shahzad clearly returned to the United States after terrorist training in Pakistan and began construction of a bomb. If we include the shoe bomber and the underwear bomber (bringing the total to 27 attackers), then two more boarded airplanes with terrorist intentions. Six others, including three U.S.-born people (Carlos Bledsoe, Edward Archer, and Rizwan Farook) and three foreigners (Tamerlan Tsarnaev, Tashfeen Malik, and Abdul Razak ali Artan) had entered or reentered the United States within a few years before the attack, although they are not known to have connected with any terrorist organization while out of the country. The remainder were U.S. citizens with no record of recent travel abroad or foreigners who had arrived in the United

States as children or many years before the attack and with no record of recent travel abroad.

Most of the foreign-born jihadists arrived in the United States when they were very young. Their average age upon arrival was 14.9 years, and the median was 16. Their average age at the time of the attack they later carried out or at the time of their arrest for plotting an attack was 27.7.[53] The median was 25. In other words, they spent an average of 12 years in the United States before planning or participating in their attacks. It is unlikely that they were sleepers or radical jihadists when they arrived—they were radicalized here.

These findings underscore the difficulty that officials face in vetting people coming into the United States. Vetting aims at uncovering those who might be pretending to be something they are not. Even the most extreme vetting cannot predict what people might believe or become many years later. To somehow look at young teenagers and forecast their behavior as twenty-somethings would require extraordinary powers to see far into the future—the bureaucratic equivalent of divine foresight.

The policy implication of these findings is that the United States needs to continue to engage in appropriate vetting of immigrants and foreign visitors, without unrealistic expectations about predictability of future behavior. At the same time, the United States must continue domestic efforts to discourage decisions to engage in violence and uncover terrorist plots.

The Complexity of Terrorist Motives Defies Easy Diagnosis

No single factor or combination of factors explains terrorist violence. Religious beliefs and jihadist ideologies play an important role but are only one component of a constellation of motives. Jihadist ideology prescribes violence as an individual duty in response to attacks on the ummah, or Muslim community. In urging people to attack enemies of the jihad wherever they are, jihadist propaganda accords warrior status to all who take action. Qasim al-Raymi, the leader of al Qaeda's affiliate in Yemen, recently told his followers in the West, "We do not view you as an individual. . . . [W]e rather view you as a group, a brigade, or even an army. . . . And it is important to view yourself from this angle."[54] It is an attractive offer that provides an opportunity to participate in an epic struggle on the side of God, membership in a brotherhood, and official recognition for one's deeds. For the true believers, joining the jihad protects one's soul against corruption, and it guarantees ascendance to paradise. But again, radicalization by itself does not automatically lead to a decision to kill.

Personal circumstances also figure heavily in the mix and, in some cases, appear to outweigh ideological grounding. Alienation, anger at perceived prejudice and injustice, avenging personal insult, the quest for identity, a feeling of emptiness, ennui, boredom, the thirst for adventure, disillusion, dissatisfaction with one's condition, personal life crises, loneliness, the need to belong—all appear in the life stories of jihadists and the various theories of radicalization. Remote recruiting via social media might be attracting those whose motives are personal.

Advertised atrocities and the prospect of unlimited violence might resonate with those already prone to aggression. Some officials believe that ISIS recruiting targets people with mental instabilities, although it is not clear how the organization identifies them—possibly through clues in their own communications.[55] Or perhaps the attribute that makes mentally unstable people promising recruits is their suggestibility.

Identifying who among foreigners applying to enter the country or those already in the United States might become terrorists in the distant future depends on a solid understanding of radicalization or recruitment to violence, which decisionmakers do not currently possess and might never possess. The imperative to prevent violence is outpacing decisionmakers' ability to predict it.

Joining Jihadist Fronts Abroad

Another manifestation of radicalization is the joining of jihadist fronts abroad. Although doing so is considered a form of providing material support to a terrorist organization, and a person can be arrested for even attempting to join a group, going abroad might actually draw off some of those who otherwise might plot terrorist attacks in the United States. ISIS has been successful in attracting fighters in other countries but less successful in the United States, where estimates of the number who have gone or attempted to go to other countries to join jihadist fronts range from 150 to 250.[56] Some of these people have been identified as a result of arrests or notices of their being killed in Syria or Iraq. Those not identified might include some still under current investigation, some whose indictments have been sealed, or some who might be cooperating with authorities. Some of those who traveled to Syria could also be members of paramilitary formations that are fighting against ISIS.

Very few of those who left the United States for Syria and Iraq have returned, and none of those who have returned from fighting in Syria or Iraq is reported to have been involved in terrorist attacks or plotting.[57] As of April 2017, we can identify 156 people who left the United States since the 1980s to join or try to join jihadist fronts abroad, including al Qaeda, the Taliban, and ISIS, or to seek foreign training and experience that could be used to plan attacks at home.[58] (Those who returned and engaged in terrorist plotting in the United States are included in numbers cited in this essay.)

Previous RAND research on 124 Americans who left or attempted to leave the United States to join or seek training with jihadist fronts abroad, including Afghanistan, Pakistan, Somalia, and Yemen, found that 40 percent were U.S.-born and 23 percent were naturalized citizens. Their average age was 25.7 years, slightly younger than the plotters examined in this essay. At least 21 percent were converts to Islam—a lower percentage than have gone or tried to go to Syria more recently.[59]

Of the 124 jihadists analyzed earlier, 33 percent were arrested before leaving the United States, 10 percent were arrested abroad, 20 percent were killed abroad, and 27 percent were arrested after their return. Ten percent were still at large when the research was done. Only nine total—or about one out of nine of those who returned—became involved in terrorism planning after they came back.[60]

Two of those who traveled abroad were involved in deadly attacks after their return: Carlos Bledsoe, a Muslim convert, who shot two American soldiers in Little Rock, Arkansas, in 2009, had spent 16 months in Yemen; and Tamerlan Tsarnaev, one of the 2013 Boston Marathon bombers, spent six months in Russia in 2012. Bledsoe claimed in prison that he had been a soldier of al Qaeda in the Arabian Peninsula, but investigators could find no evidence that he had ever connected with the terrorist organization, and there were some doubts about his mental condition. Although Russian authorities were aware of Tsarnaev, there is again no evidence that he connected with any terrorist organization while abroad.

It might be too early to assess whether American fighters returning from Syria will pose a greater threat than the previous cohorts who traveled abroad to join jihadist fronts in Afghanistan, Pakistan, Somalia, Yemen, or elsewhere. Only a few of those made it to Syria, most of them presumably to join ISIS or other jihadist groups; only a handful are known to have returned to the United States. The number of returnees publicly identified as a result of arrests is well short of the number that American officials have publicly estimated went or tried to go to Syria. Presumably, officials know their identities, but they might be subjects of ongoing investigations or sealed indictments.

The number of Americans who have attempted to join ISIS in Syria is a small fraction of those who have gone to Syria from Europe, especially from France, Belgium, Germany, and the UK.[61] European authorities face far greater volumes of returning jihadists, and, as the terrorist campaigns in France and Belgium indicate, returning fighters to these two countries have been able to connect with local confederates. The returning jihadists come from deeply embedded subcultures within immigrant communities.[62] Although returning European fighters could pose an indirect threat to the United States, making cooperation with European security services crucial, Europe's unique history and circumstances are not an appropriate model for assessing the threat posed by returning American fighters.

The number of Americans who have attempted to join ISIS in Syria is a small fraction of those who have gone to Syria from Europe, especially from France, Belgium, Germany, and the UK.

A more detailed analysis of those going abroad to join jihadist groups, as well as those convicted of providing other forms of material support but not plotting terrorist attacks in the United States, is forthcoming. In my previous research, I have included people in these two categories.[63] This material is currently being updated and will appear in future publications.

Most foreign-born terrorists radicalize after arrival in the United States. Few of the terrorist plotters arrived within the past 15 years. Most have lived here for many years. And most arrived as children.

Conclusions and Policy Implications

Only a small number of Americans are willing to carry out jihadist terrorist attacks in the United States. The numbers of attackers and plotters cited in this essay are not a representative sample of a larger population—they comprise the entire universe, according to the criteria described in the appendix. Changing the criteria to include those cases involving Muslim defendants but in which authorities believe that jihadist ideology was not involved and cases in which defendants were acquitted in the courts or were found to be mentally incompetent to stand trial will add some names, but not many. This suggests that jihadist ideology has found little resonance among America's Muslim communities, that the FBI and police have been successful in deterring terrorist activity by uncovering and thwarting most terrorist attacks and in preventing jihadists from organizing groups capable of sustaining a terrorist campaign, and that, since 9/11, measures aimed at deterring or preventing jihadist terrorists from infiltrating the country have been largely successful.

Nonetheless, radicalization is taking place here, and it involves both U.S.- and foreign-born persons. Foreign jihadist groups have not been able to incite many to terrorist violence; homegrown terrorists remain the principal threat.

Most foreign-born terrorists radicalize after arrival in the United States. Few of the terrorist plotters arrived within the past 15 years. Most have lived here for many years. And most arrived as children.

The arrival ages of those who later plotted terrorist attacks show a discernible cluster around 16 years of age, indicating a possible assimilation problem for a few. However, it is no more than a handful of people.

Another portion of the jihadists are second-generation immigrants. The radicalization of these people recalls a phenomenon seen in other terrorist groups that pursued foreign quarrels—for example, the anti-Castro Cuban extremists responsible for bombings in the Miami area during the 1970s and South Moluccan extremists responsible for hostage incidents in the Netherlands during the same decade. In other words, jihadist radicalization might not be that different from other forms of radicalization. Identity issues, the quest for glory, and the lure of imagined utopias—whether a restoration of pre-Castro Cuba, an independent South Molucca, an Islamic caliphate, or youthful rebellion against immigrant parents who have focused on economic survival—offer possible explanations.

Islam is a growing religion, but converts seem to be overrepresented among jihadist plotters. Again, this might reflect the fervent embrace of newly acquired beliefs or perhaps that the convert has not been fully socialized in the new beliefs. In either case, it is not clear that there is a policy solution.

Reviewing how the trajectory of jihadist groups abroad could affect the threat of future terrorist action in the United States should be an ongoing effort. New measures that reflect new threats could become necessary. However, the recently proposed restrictions on entries from certain specified countries, had they constituted a permanent ban since 9/11, would have had only a marginal effect on jihadist terrorist activity in the United States.

Nationality is a poor indicator of future terrorist activity. An analysis by DHS of 82 jihadists identified since 2011 concluded that country of origin was not a reliable indicator of a terrorist threat.[64] According to the DHS statistics, slightly more than half of those identified were born in the United States. The others came from 26 countries, none of which accounted for more than 13.5 percent of the foreign-born total. Very few entrants from the seven countries named in the first version of the proposed immigration restriction were involved in U.S.-based terrorist attacks.

The numbers compiled for this essay underscore the DHS findings. Of the 178 people who participated in carrying out or plotting terrorist attacks since 9/11, at least 48 percent were born in the United States. The remainder came from 38 countries, most of them having a Muslim majority.[65]

The vetting enhancements recently proposed by the Department of State, including examining applicants' social media activity, could help uncover existing terrorists attempting to infiltrate the United Sates but will provide few clues regarding the future beliefs or behavior of young immigrants more than a decade after their arrival.

The patterns of radicalization appear to be changing. The process could be accelerating, but it is difficult to track the trajectory of individual radicalization with any confidence. Recent recruits tend to be younger than previous recruits. Their lives appear more disordered. It is not clear whether this reflects greater reliance on remote recruiting through social media or a profile of those most likely to fall prey to police undercover operations.

Publicly reported numbers suggest that thousands of investigations have been conducted since 9/11, but there have been only a handful of arrests each year. Thus, many investigations must conclude that the subject or subjects being investigated pose no threat. We do not know how many people come close to action (or to the attention of investigators) and then back away. People come onto and fall off the radar. We know only about those who are arrested. We know nothing about those who drop out, except that, on occasion, they might show up in a subsequent plot.

Some of those who engaged in jihadist terrorist attacks had previously come to the attention of federal authorities. Several of them were interviewed by FBI officials, in some cases only months before carrying out an attack, and were judged not to be dangerous. No criticism is intended—the assessment might have been correct at the time. Large numbers come to the attention of the authorities; few ever act. The public and political leadership have to accept that predicting dangerousness is extremely difficult.

With so few jihadists overall, many of whom are lone offenders or recent converts, it is fair to ask whether community programs to counter violent extremism are likely to affect recruitment to violence and the number of terrorist plots? The complexity of motives and the idiosyncratic combinations seen in the brief biographies of American jihadists suggest some skepticism of the nation's ability to prevent violent extremism.

Past studies indicate that terrorists are no more likely to suffer from mental illness than the general population, yet it has become increasingly difficult to distinguish ideologically driven terrorists from mentally unstable people for whom the ideology seems to have become a conveyer of personal discontents.[66] This is not an argument that terrorism can be dismissed as a manifestation of mental illness or that mentally ill persons are prone to terrorism. The troubled nature of the biographies of recent terrorist plotters could reflect a certain type of person who is attracted by the current jihadist recruiting themes. It might also reflect the "recruiting" process itself, in which ISIS seeks to remotely inspire people to take action and publicly awards "membership" and accolades to anyone who does. The Internet has also made jihadist terrorism an increasingly solitary activity. Inspiring people to violence is very different from recruiting people into an organization.

The very small number of jihadist plotters makes it difficult to generalize about their mental health, mind-set, or motives. That they are so few in number is good news for the nation. And few come from abroad. They radicalize often years after their arrival. The reasons are complex. They are dangerous people, like any mad bomber or mass shooter, but an unreceptive community, good intelligence, and effective law enforcement thus far have constrained their violence.

Appendix

Chronology of Jihadist Attacks and Plots in the United States, September 2001–April 2017

The numbers mentioned in this essay derive from the cases listed below. These include 20 terrorist attacks (not counting the foreign-based attempts to sabotage U.S.-bound airliners) and 86 plots motivated by jihadist ideology and aimed at the U.S. homeland. They involve Americans as the principal actors or conspirators or as confederates, inspired by or assisting a foreign terrorist organization in an actual plot to carry out an attack in the United States.

What's In and What's Out

Excluded from the chronology are those cases involving only material support to jihadist organizations abroad—sending money, weapons, or equipment or assisting in propaganda. (This group is the subject of separate research.) In some of the plots below, however, the participants were prosecuted for providing material support and not the actual plot. This could reflect the quality of the evidence of an actual plot or negotiations to reduce charges in return for a guilty plea.

The focus of this essay is "homegrown terrorism," attacks planned and prepared in the United States. Therefore, the chronology excludes foreign plots to attack the U.S. homeland in which there is no nexus with domestic operatives or confederates. This means, for example, omitting the 2001 shoe bomber, a UK national, and the 2009 underwear bomber, a Nigerian national, both of whom were recruited and equipped with their bombs abroad. For the same reasons, the chronology also excludes a plot discovered by Lebanese authorities in 2006 to carry out attacks on the PATH commuter train tunnel beneath the Hudson River between New Jersey and New York. The leader of the plot arrested in Lebanon was a Lebanese national who had visited the United States six years before. No Americans were ever identified as part of the plot, and no preparations were made in the United States. In 2006, UK authorities uncovered a plot to smuggle liquid explosives aboard U.S.-bound flights from Heathrow Airport in London. Again, this was an attack planned and prepared abroad—no Americans were involved, so I have also excluded this plot.

The chronology also excludes cases in which people left or tried to leave the United States to obtain terrorist training or join a jihadist front abroad, even if that meant that they could be operating against American forces overseas. (This group also is the subject of previous and forthcoming research.) However, I do include those who went abroad from the United States and then returned to plot terrorist operations in the United States. Eventually, these three categories of terrorists and terrorist supporters—those who provided material support, those who left or tried to leave the country to join jihadist fronts abroad, and those who carried out or plotted to carry out attacks in the United States—will be brought together for comparison.

These criteria sound straightforward, but, invariably, there are gray areas and judgment calls.

Chronologies of jihadist terrorist plots can be contentious. There is no single charge of terrorism that legally defines what should be included or excluded. Defendants in the cases listed below have been charged with violation of a variety of federal terrorism statutes, often the material-support statutes (18 U.S.C. §§ 2339A, 2339B, and 2339C) and use of weapons of mass destruction (18 U.S.C. § 2332A), as well as other, more-general offenses, including lying to investigators. The aim of U.S. authorities is to deter and disrupt terrorism plots at a very early stage through prosecution, using whatever legal tools can be mobilized. Some of the prosecutions have taken place in state courts or military courts, where different terms and different laws apply.

Some of the plots included below seem far-fetched, way beyond the capabilities of the perpetrators, but the federal statutes allow for prosecution on the basis of intentions—a commitment to carry out a terrorist attack as opposed to actually attempting to carry it out. Demonstrated capabilities are not a requirement of guilt. In some cases, the authorities provided what the defendant believed to be the means of attack—for example, a fake bomb.

Whether the act was intended to achieve political goals, which makes it terrorism, requires assessing motives, which can be complex. The boundaries between political objectives, personal motives, and mental instability are not well defined. The people included here were motivated by a mixture of ideological fanaticism, desires for personal revenge against the government for perceived injustices, or personal grievances unrelated to any political cause. Mental instabilities also figure in the mix. Although it is often difficult to determine whether the intended action was motivated primarily by ideology or by other factors, I have tried to include only those cases in which there is an indication that jihadist beliefs propelled the plot. The absence of any apparent jihadist component argued for exclusion.

My own efforts to compile an empirical history of jihadist terrorism in the United States in the years since the 9/11 attacks began in preparation for testimony before the U.S. Senate Committee on Homeland Security after the 2009 Fort Hood shooting. I relied on U.S. Department of Justice and FBI public announcements and news media. Since then, other researchers have published chronologies, which I have consulted in preparing this one.[67] It is noteworthy that no two chronologies agree exactly on the total number of attacks and plots.

In deciding what should be included in a chronology of "terrorist" plots, each author must make some judgments of his or her own. This is perilous. Inclusiveness can be criticized as branding every Muslim criminal a terrorist, thereby exaggerating the danger. Omissions bring accusations of trying to minimize the jihadist threat. Given this environment, I have tried to be completely transparent about my reasons for including or excluding a particular case.

I have leaned toward inclusiveness—relatively few cases have been deliberately omitted, even though, in my personal view, the seriousness of some of the plots is questionable. I offer no independent judgment as to whether any specific plot was real, whether political aims were the primary motive in every single case, or whether justice was done—these are separate discussions. Readers ultimately must decide for themselves.

For obvious reasons, I excluded defendants found not guilty. I have omitted those cases in which the perpetrator might have been Muslim but there is no evidence that jihadist ideology motivated the attack. This is probably the biggest source of difference among the various chronologies.

Also omitted here are those cases in which defendants were judged to be mentally incompetent to stand trial. This is not to assert that terrorists cannot also suffer from some degree of mental disorder. No doubt some do, but lone offenders, with histories of mental illness, listening to disembodied voices or exhibiting other manifestations of being unable to distinguish reality, in my view, ought not be regarded as politically motivated terrorists. Some of those whom courts have found to be mentally incompetent to stand trial appear on other lists of jihadist plotters.

Examples of some of the deliberate omissions include John Allen Muhammad and Lee Boyd Malvo, who were convicted of the 2002 Northern Virginia sniper attacks in which ten people died. I excluded Joel Henry Hinrichs III; the FBI found no connection to any political cause.

I omitted Omeed Aziz Popal and Ali R. Warrayat, both responsible for car rammings in 2006: Warrayat's motives were described as personal and, in any case, both Warrayat and Popal were judged to be legally insane. Clifford L. Cousins, who made threats against the President in 2003; Tahmeed Ahmed, who assaulted a government employee in 2007; Joshua Ryne Goldberg, arrested in a 2015 bomb plot; and Adel Daoud, arrested in a 2016 Chicago bomb plot, were all found mentally incompetent.

The case of Esteban Santiago-Ruiz, who was responsible for a 2017 shooting attack at the Fort Lauderdale Airport in which five people were killed and six wounded, is still before the court. Santiago-Ruiz, an army veteran, had earlier complained to the FBI that the government was forcing him to watch terrorist videos and that the Central Intelligence Agency was forcing him to join ISIS. He also said that he heard voices in his head telling him to commit acts of violence. Because several of those involved in jihadist terrorist attacks or plots have (or claim in their own defense) histories of mental illness, I have omitted only those whom the court has deemed mentally unfit.

It was a judgment call not to include two people recently arrested until more details are available about their cases. One is Gregory Lepsky, who was arrested in May 2017. A U.S.-born convert to Islam, he stabbed the family dog and, while being treated by paramedics for injuries to his arm and without being questioned, announced to police that he intended to kill his mother and that he was a member of ISIS and was about to leave for Turkey. Placed in custody and taken to the hospital for additional treatment, he further volunteered the information that he was going to make a pressure-cooker bomb and intended to kill people in New York.[68] Although he has been charged with material support, no further details were available at the time of writing. The second person is Amor M. Ftouhi, a dual Moroccan-Canadian citizen who, in late June 2017, stabbed a police officer at Bishop International Airport in Flint, Michigan. According to statements Ftouhi made at the time of the assault, it appears to be a jihad-motivated attack, but, at the time of writing, insufficient information was available and the case has not been included here.

Finally, I have omitted several cases involving so-called honor killings, cases in which a father killed his daughter because she rejected an arranged marriage or was dating a non-Muslim or a husband killing his wife who wanted a divorce, and several incidents labeled as hate crimes—every Muslim murderer is not a terrorist. Again, these are judgment calls. Putting aside deliberate omissions, no claim can be made that every case has been captured.

Comparison with Other Lists

I compared the cases and names included in this chronology with the lists compiled by New America/Bergen et al.,[69] *Daily Signal*/Walters,[70] Triangle Center on Terrorism and Homeland Security/Kurzman,[71] and Mershon Center for International Security Studies/Mueller.[72] These four cover the entire period addressed in this essay. Recognizing that each analysis follows different criteria, the objective of the comparison was to determine the degree of overlap between the data presented here and those included in the other lists. How many of the people on this list also appear on the other lists? Alternatively, how many of those included on the other lists do not appear this list?

The New America/Bergen list includes 167 (or 94 percent) of the 178 names on the list used for this essay. Making the comparison in the other direction is not easily done because the New America/Bergen list of 407 names is all-inclusive. In addition to those who plotted or carried out attacks, it contains those charged solely with providing material support, those who attempted to join jihadist fronts abroad, and foreigners involved in foreign plots against the United States. The latter three categories are not addressed here.

The *Daily Signal*/Walters list of terrorist attacks and plots includes 152 (or 85 percent) of the names on my list, as well as 16 names not on my list. (In other words, my list contains 90 percent of the names on the Walters list.) These 16 names include the so-called Lackawanna Six, a group of Yemeni Americans who traveled to Afghanistan before 9/11. Frightened by the experience, the six returned to the United States after some weeks. (A seventh remained committed and was later arrested in Yemen.) The six returnees were arrested in 2002. Although described in some news media as a "sleeper cell," they engaged in no terrorist plotting and were charged only with material support of terrorism for briefly training with al Qaeda. The Lackawanna Six appear in the other chronologies as well.

In addition to the Lackawanna Six, Walters includes several others involved only in material support, not terrorist plotting; four people whom my list omits because they were found not guilty; and one person found to be legally insane. Most of the remaining people were foreigners involved in foreign terrorist plots.

Kurzman's list matches 156 (or 88 percent) of the names on my list and has 30 names not on my list—my list therefore has 84 percent of those on Kurzman's list. I omitted the 30 from my list because their actions appear to fall more in the realm of simply communicating a threat rather than plotting an attack, the actions had no clear nexus with jihadist motives, or the person was found to be legally insane.

Mueller's list matches 109 (or 61 percent) of the names on my list and has seven names not on my list, meaning that my list has 94 percent of those on Mueller's list. The same reasons for my decision to omit these apply: They were acquitted, were found mentally incompetent, or were foreigners involved in foreign plots.

Comparing the other lists with mine also offered the opportunity to review the cases listed by others but that were not on my list in order, first, to ensure against missing anyone through oversight and, second, to reconsider my reasons for omitting them. This resulted in a few additions. Overall, the four lists overlap by around 85 percent, with the differences being explained almost entirely by the criteria described above.

Notes

[1] U.S. Department of Justice, Office of the Inspector General, *The September 11 Detainees: A Review of the Treatment of Aliens Held on Immigration Charges in Connection with the Investigation of the September 11 Attacks*, Washington, D.C., April 2003.

[2] Maia Jachimowicz and Ramah McKay, "'Special Registration' Program," Migration Policy Institute, April 1, 2003.

[3] David Cole, *Enemy Aliens: Double Standards and Constitutional Freedoms in the War on Terrorism*, New York: New Press, 2003. Cole includes among the five Earnest James Ujaama, a U.S. citizen, who was detained as a material witness and subsequently charged with planning to establish a terrorist training camp to support al Qaeda in the United States. However, all charges were dropped except one in exchange for Ujaama's pleading guilty to providing economic aid to the Taliban. (His name is included in earlier RAND research: Brian Michael Jenkins, *Stray Dogs and Virtual Armies: Radicalization and Recruitment to Jihadist Terrorism in the United States Since 9/11*, Santa Monica, Calif.: RAND Corporation, OP-343-RC, 2011.) Four more men were arrested in Detroit as part of a "sleeper cell" and charged with supporting terrorist activity. One of them was acquitted of all charges, one was convicted of visa fraud, and two others were convicted of providing support to a terrorist group. However, the charges against all three were subsequently overturned in a new trial owing to false accusations, possible perjury, misleading and withheld evidence, and prosecutorial misconduct. See Maurice Possley, "Ahmed Hannan," National Registry of Exonerations, undated.

[4] Eric T. Schneiderman, attorney general, State of New York, letter to President Barack Obama urging the President to rescind the National Security Entry–Exit Registration System regulatory framework, December 19, 2016.

[5] This was José Padilla, a U.S.-born convert to Islam who traveled to Afghanistan to join al Qaeda in 2001. He was sent back to the United States to plan and carry out a terrorist mission but was arrested at the airport and later convicted of terrorism.

[6] Brian Michael Jenkins and Joseph Trella, *Carnage Interrupted: An Analysis of Fifteen Terrorist Plots Against Public Surface Transportation*, San Jose, Calif.: Mineta Transportation Institute, April 2012. No arrests were made, and very little is known about this plot. According to reported intelligence intercepts, al Qaeda's then–second-in-command called it off for something better.

[7] Jenkins and Trella, 2012. According to Lebanese authorities, a group of terrorists in Lebanon led by Assam Hammoud, a Lebanese jihadist volunteer, planned to detonate backpack bombs on PATH trains while under the Hudson River between New Jersey and New York. The plotters discussed the amount of explosives required to breach the tunnel lining, which would flood the tunnel, underground stations in Lower Manhattan, and other below-sea-level tunnels.

[8] These plots and the Padilla plot noted above are described in the appendix.

[9] By *homegrown*, I mean terrorist plots that primarily U.S. residents planned and prepared in the United States as opposed to being carried out by foreigners recruited abroad to infiltrate the country and carry out an attack, as was the case with the 9/11 hijackers and the shoe bomber. *Homegrown* does not exclude cases in which Americans were inspired by jihadist propaganda or urged to action by terrorist communicators abroad or those cases in which Americans joined terrorist groups abroad to obtain training and then returned with the expectation that they would carry out an attack.

[10] White House, "Remarks by the President at the Summit on Countering Violent Extremism," February 19, 2015b.

[11] Economic and Social Research Council, "Prevent: UK's Counter Terrorism Strategy," undated. See also UK Ministry of Justice, *Policy Paper: 2010 to 2015 Government Policy: Counter-Terrorism*, May 8, 2015.

[12] Supporting legislation was introduced in the Senate, but the initiative aroused strong objections from civil libertarians and no such commission was ever created. For an additional view, see Brian Michael Jenkins, *Defining the Role of a National Commission on the Prevention of Violent Extremism and Homegrown Terrorism*, testimony before the U.S. House of Representatives Committee on Homeland Security Subcommittee on Intelligence, Information Sharing, and Terrorism Risk Assessment, June 14, 2007, Santa Monica, Calif.: RAND Corporation, CT-285, 2007.

[13] White House, *Empowering Local Partners to Prevent Violent Extremism in the United States*, Washington, D.C., August 2011.

[14] Jerome P. Bjelopera, *Countering Violent Extremism in the United States*, Washington, D.C.: Congressional Research Service, February 19, 2014. See also Lorenzo Vidino and Seamus Hughes, *Countering Violent Extremism in America*, Washington, D.C.: Center for Cyber and Homeland Security, George Washington University, June 2015a.

[15] This had obvious implications for civil liberties. See Karen J. Greenberg, *Rogue Justice: The Making of the Security State*, New York: Crown Publishers, 2016a.

[16] White House, "Fact Sheet: The White House Summit on Countering Violent Extremism," February 18, 2015a.

[17] Brett McGurk, special presidential envoy for the Global Coalition to Counter ISIL, U.S. Department of State, "Update on Campaign Against ISIL," briefing, October 7, 2016.

[18] "15 Years After 9/11, a Sharp Partisan Divide on Ability of Terrorists to Strike U.S.," *U.S. Politics and Policy*, Pew Research Center, September 7, 2016.

[19] Miranda Green, "Homeland Security Chief: Airplane Terror Threat 'Keeps Me Up at Night,'" CNN Politics, April 28, 2017.

[20] The U.S. Department of Defense controversially classified the Fort Hood shooting as an incident of workplace violence, provoking criticism from those who saw it as an attempt to minimize jihadist terrorism in the United States, while the Senate called it an act of terrorism. The administration classified it as terrorism in 2015, making its victims eligible for the Purple Heart.

[21] Brian Michael Jenkins and Bruce R. Butterworth, *The Threat to Air and Ground Transportation Posed by Mentally Disordered Assailants*, San Jose, Calif.: Mineta Transportation Institute, March 2017.

[22] U.S. Department of Homeland Security, "Home and Away: DHS and the Threats to America, Remarks delivered by Secretary Kelly at George Washington University Center for Cyber and Homeland Security," released April 18, 2017a. As of October 18, 2017:
https://www.dhs.gov/news/2017/04/18/home-and-away-dhs-and-threats-america

[23] Michael Lipka, "Muslims and Islam: Key Findings in the U.S. and Around the World," *Fact Tank: News in the Numbers*, Pew Research Center, February 27, 2017.

[24] DHS, "Yearbook of Immigration Statistics 2015," last published May 16, 2017b.

[25] Bureau of Consular Affairs, U.S. Department of State, "Immigrant Visas Issued at Foreign Service Posts (by Foreign State Chargeability) (All Categories) Fiscal Years 2007–2016," undated (a).

[26] Jens Manuel Krogstad and Jynnah Radford, "Key Facts About Refugees to the U.S.," *Fact Tank: News in the Numbers*, Pew Research Center, January 30, 2017.

[27] DHS, 2017b; Bureau of Consular Affairs, U.S. Department of State, "Nonimmigrant Visa Statistics," undated (b).

[28] The 3 million figure excludes India, the country of origin of two plotters. India alone accounted for 1.8 million of the 5 million nonimmigrant visas issued in 2015.

[29] DHS, 2017b.

[30] Jenkins, 2011.

[31] I mention these two only to examine the record of the Visa Waiver Program over its entire history. I do not include them among the 87 who came from abroad in the current study because the latter figure refers only to those involved in post-9/11 attacks or plots. Both arrived in the United States and were arrested prior to 9/11.

[32] Ahmed Ajaj was born in the West Bank in 1966 and immigrated to the United States sometime in the late 1980s. In 1992, he left the United States to join al Qaeda. He received training in bomb-building and attempted to return to the United States on a crudely altered Swedish passport, a visa-waiver country. His passport attracted attention at the airport, and he was sent for a secondary inspection, during which officials found other passports and bomb-making instructions. He was arrested at the airport and spent six months in jail but, while incarcerated, assisted in the planning of the 1993 World Trade Center bombing. He was released from detention five days after the bombing, but investigators discovered his involvement and he was rearrested eight days later.

[33] Although Moussaoui, who was born in France, is sometimes referred to as the 20th hijacker, it is not clear that he was actually intended to play a role in the 9/11 attacks. He might have been involved in a separate terrorist plot, lending credence to the perception that al Qaeda had infiltrated sleepers into the United States.

[34] Although a UK citizen, Richard Reid's criminal record and lengthy period of time in Afghanistan and subsequent travel patterns would presumably flag him as a risk today, if such information were available to U.S. intelligence.

[35] Pew Research Center, *Muslim Americans: Middle Class and Mostly Mainstream—War on Terror Concerns*, Washington, D.C., May 22, 2007; Pew Research Center, *Muslim Americans: No Signs of Growth in Alienation or Support for Extremism*, Washington, D.C., August 30, 2011.

[36] Pew Research Center, 2011.

[37] Pew Research Center, 2011.

[38] Patrick Hennessy and Melissa Kite, "Poll Reveals 40pc of Muslims Want Sharia Law in UK," *Telegraph*, February 19, 2006.

[39] GfK NOP Social Research, *Attitudes to Living in Britain: Topline Findings*, April 27, 2006.

[40] Pew Research Center, 2011.

[41] Pew Research Center, 2007.

[42] Richard Wike and Greg Smith, "Little Support for Terrorism Among Muslim Americans," Washington, D.C.: Pew Research Center, December 17, 2009.

[43] Pew Research Center, 2007.

[44] Kim Cragin, Melissa A. Bradley, Eric Robinson, and Paul S. Steinberg, *What Factors Cause Youth to Reject Violent Extremism? Results of an Exploratory Analysis in the West Bank*, Santa Monica, Calif.: RAND Corporation, RR-1118-CMEPP, 2015, p. 16; Jamie Bartlett and Carl Miller, "The Edge of Violence: Towards Telling the Difference Between Violent and Non-Violent Radicalization," *Terrorism and Political Violence*, Vol. 24, No. 1, 2012, pp. 1–21, makes a similar point.

[45] Rachel Weiner, "20-Year-Old Says He Planned ISIS Terror Attacks in Virginia, North Carolina," *Washington Post*, November 29, 2016.

[46] The total number of plots is subject to interpretation. Some analyses include as terrorist plots cases involving material support for terrorist organizations, including financing, attempting to acquire weapons and other equipment, and assistance in propaganda efforts, as well cases involving joining or attempting to join terrorist groups abroad. Even when plots are more narrowly defined as plans to carry out actual attacks in the United States, differences still arise, although they are smaller. For example, the Heritage Foundation's compilation of "Islamist terror plots" in the United States as of February 2017 ran to 95 plots, including the shoe bomber and the underwear bomber. John Mueller, ed., *Terrorism Since 9/11: The American Cases*, Columbus, Ohio: Ohio State University, Mershon Center for International

Security Studies, January 2017, lists 92 cases, although some of these involve people whose ultimate aim is to fight abroad.

[47] "Home and Away: DHS and the Threats to America, Remarks Delivered by Secretary Kelly at George Washington University Center for Cyber and Homeland Security," U.S. Department of Homeland Security, April 18, 2017.

[48] Jenkins, 2011.

[49] Charles Kurzman, *Muslim-American Involvement with Violent Extremism, 2016*, Chapel Hill, N.C.: Triangle Center on Terrorism and Homeland Security, January 26, 2017. According to Kurzman, 35 percent of Muslim Americans connected with violent extremism since 9/11 are converts. According to Vidino and Hughes, approximately 40 percent of ISIS recruits in the United States are converts. The percentage of converts seems to be increasing and might reflect ISIS's broader reach via social media and recruiting messaging (Lorenzo Vidino and Seamus Hughes, *ISIS in America: From Retweets to Raqqa*, Washington, D.C.: George Washington University Program on Extremism, December 2015b).

[50] "Converts to Islam," *Fact Tank: News in the Numbers*, Pew Research Center, July 21, 2007.

[51] As of 2009, 43.7 percent of the immigrants living in the United States had become U.S. citizens (Jeanne Batalova and Aaron Terrazas, "Frequently Requested Statistics on Immigrants and Immigration in the United States," Washington, D.C.: Migration Policy Institute, December 9, 2010).

[52] See the appendix for a more detailed description of the plotters.

[53] This was the average age only of those 66 people whose age upon arrival we also know. The average age at the time of attack or arrest for all foreign-born terrorist attackers and plotters, as mentioned previously, was 29.3.

[54] Thomas Joscelyn, "AQAP Leader Calls for 'Simple' Attacks in the West," *FDD's Long War Journal*, May 8, 2017.

[55] Tom Porter, "Isis Targeting Misfits and Mentally Ill to Commit Lone-Wolf Terror Attacks, Claims UK Police Chief," *International Business Times*, undated.

[56] Nicholas J. Rasmussen, director, National Counterterrorism Center, "Countering Violent Islamist Extremism: The Urgent Threat of Foreign Fighters and Homegrown Terror," testimony before the U.S. House of Representatives Committee on Homeland Security, February 11, 2015. The director of the National Counterterrorism Center put the estimate at more than 150 but indicated that it was impossible to be precise. FBI director Comey put the number of those who have gone or tried to go to Syria at 250 (James B. Comey, director, Federal Bureau of Investigation, "Threats to the Homeland," statement before the U.S. Senate Committee on Homeland Security and Governmental Affairs, October 8, 2015).

[57] In November 2015, Senator Jeff Sessions released a list of 12 people admitted to the United States as refugees who were subsequently involved in terrorism-related crimes. The charges were for aiding or attempting to join jihadist groups abroad. None was involved in a domestic terrorist plot (Investigative Project on Terrorism, *America's Refugee, Asylum, and Visa Waiver Programs: Our Entire Access System Is Broken*, undated [b]).

[58] This is an update of the original total in Brian Michael Jenkins, "When Jihadis Come Marching Home," *Hill*, November 19, 2014.

[59] Jenkins, 2014.

[60] Jenkins, 2014.

[61] Bibi van Ginkel and Eva Entenmann, eds., *The Foreign Fighters Phenomenon in the European Union: Profiles, Threats and Policies*, The Hague: International Centre for Counter-Terrorism, April 2016. These four countries, which contain about 44 percent of the European Union's total population, account for more than three-quarters of the foreign fighters.

[62] See Giles Kepel and Antoine Jardin, *Terror in France: The Rise of Jihad in the West*, Princeton, N.J.: Princeton Studies in Muslim Politics, 2017. The subculture that produced the foreign fighters and homegrown extremists responsible for the recent terrorist campaign in France and Belgium is also discussed in Brian Michael Jenkins and Jean-François Clair, *Trains, Concert Halls, Airports, and Restaurants—All Soft Targets: What the Terrorist Campaign in France and Belgium Tells Us About the Future of Jihadist Terrorism in Europe*, San Jose, Calif.: Mineta Transportation Institute, Report WP 12-10, June 2016.

[63] Jenkins, 2011; Jenkins, 2014.

[64] The draft DHS memorandum, DHS, Acting Under Secretary for Intelligence and Analysis, "Citizenship Likely an Unreliable Indicator of Terrorist Threat to the United States," undated, was leaked to the Associated Press, which posted it online. The Associated Press story appears as Vivian Salama and Alicia A. Caldwell, "AP Exclusive: DHS Report Disputes Threat from Banned Nations," Associated Press, February 24, 2017.

[65] Salama and Caldwell, 2017.

[66] Carlos Bledsoe, Nidal Hasan, Tamerlan Tsarnaev, Elton Simpson, Mohammad Youssuf Abdulazeez, and Omar Mateen were all identified as possibly having connections to terrorism prior to their attacks.

[67] Emily Corner and Paul Gill, "Is There a Nexus Between Terrorist Involvement and Mental Health in the Age of the Islamic State?" *CTC Sentinel*, Vol. 10, No. 1, January 23, 2017, pp. 1–10; Jenkins and Clair, 2016. Some studies of European fighters suggest a much higher indication of mental illness. See van Ginkel and Entenmann, 2016.

[68] In addition to news releases by the FBI and the U.S. Department of Justice and news media accounts, I have used the following sources: Peter Bergen, Albert Ford, Alyssa Sims, and David Sterman, *Terrorism in America After 9/11*, New America, undated; Steven Bucci, James Carafano, and Jessica Zuckerman, *60 Terrorist Plots Since 9/11: Continued Lessons in Domestic Counterterrorism*, Heritage Foundation, July 22, 2013 (Riley Walters, "An Interactive Timeline of the 85 Islamist Terror Plots Since 9/11," *Daily Signal*, May 16, 2016, has updated the Heritage Foundation data used here); Karen J. Greenberg, ed., *Case by Case: ISIS Prosecutions in the United States, March 1, 2014–June 30, 2016*, Center on National Security at Fordham Law, July 2016b (Investigative Project on Terrorism, home page, undated [a], contains many of the original court documents on most of the cases); Kurzman, 2017 (earlier versions of Kurzman's chronologies have also been posted online); Mueller, 2017 (this source provides the most detailed account of the cases); and U.S. House of Representatives Committee on Homeland Security, "Terror Threat Snapshot," undated (these are monthly updates posted on the committee's website).

[69] Criminal Complaint, *U.S. v. Lepsky*, D.N.J., May 4, 2017 (Magistrate 17-8071).

[70] Bergen et al., undated.

[71] Walters, 2016.

[72] Kurzman, 2017.

[73] Mueller, 2017.

[74] Mueller, 2017, provides the most detailed analysis of this case.

References

"15 Years After 9/11, a Sharp Partisan Divide on Ability of Terrorists to Strike U.S.," *U.S. Politics and Policy*, Pew Research Center, September 7, 2016. As of August 30, 2017: http://www.people-press.org/2016/09/07/15-years-after-911-a-sharp-partisan-divide-on-ability-of-terrorists-to-strike-u-s/

Bartlett, Jamie, and Carl Miller, "The Edge of Violence: Towards Telling the Difference Between Violent and Non-Violent Radicalization," *Terrorism and Political Violence*, Vol. 24, No. 1, 2012, pp. 1–21.

Batalova, Jeanne, and Aaron Terrazas, "Frequently Requested Statistics on Immigrants and Immigration in the United States," Washington, D.C.: Migration Policy Institute, December 9, 2010. As of August 30, 2017: http://www.migrationpolicy.org/article/frequently-requested-statistics-immigrants-and-immigration-united-states-1

Bergen, Peter, Albert Ford, Alyssa Sims, and David Sterman, *Terrorism in America After 9/11*, New America, undated. As of August 30, 2017: https://www.newamerica.org/in-depth/terrorism-in-america/

Bjelopera, Jerome P., *Countering Violent Extremism in the United States*, Washington, D.C.: Congressional Research Service, February 19, 2014. As of August 30, 2017: https://fas.org/sgp/crs/homesec/R42553.pdf

Bucci, Steven, James Carafano, and Jessica Zuckerman, *60 Terrorist Plots Since 9/11: Continued Lessons in Domestic Counterterrorism*, Heritage Foundation, July 22, 2013. As of August 30, 2017: http://www.heritage.org/terrorism/report/60-terrorist-plots-911-continued-lessons-domestic-counterterrorism

Bureau of Consular Affairs, U.S. Department of State, "Immigrant Visas Issued at Foreign Service Posts (by Foreign State Chargeability) (All Categories) Fiscal Years 2007–2016," undated (a). As of August 30, 2017: https://travel.state.gov/content/dam/visas/Statistics/AnnualReports/FY2016AnnualReport/FY16AnnualReport-TableXIV.pdf

———, "Nonimmigrant Visa Statistics," undated (b). As of August 31, 2017: https://travel.state.gov/content/visas/en/law-and-policy/statistics/non-immigrant-visas.html

Cole, David, *Enemy Aliens: Double Standards and Constitutional Freedoms in the War on Terrorism*, New York: New Press, 2003.

Comey, James B., director, Federal Bureau of Investigation, "Threats to the Homeland," statement before the U.S. Senate Committee on Homeland Security and Governmental Affairs, October 8, 2015. As of August 30, 2017: https://www.fbi.gov/news/testimony/threats-to-the-homeland

"Converts to Islam," *Fact Tank: News in the Numbers*, Pew Research Center, July 21, 2007. As of August 30, 2017: http://www.pewresearch.org/fact-tank/2007/07/21/converts-to-islam/

Corner, Emily, and Paul Gill, "Is There a Nexus Between Terrorist Involvement and Mental Health in the Age of the Islamic State?" *CTC Sentinel*, Vol. 10, No. 1, January 23, 2017, pp. 1–10. As of August 30, 2017: https://www.ctc.usma.edu/posts/is-there-a-nexus-between-terrorist-involvement-and-mental-health-in-the-age-of-the-islamic-state

Cragin, Kim, Melissa A. Bradley, Eric Robinson, and Paul S. Steinberg, *What Factors Cause Youth to Reject Violent Extremism? Results of an Exploratory Analysis in the West Bank*, Santa Monica, Calif.: RAND Corporation, RR-1118-CMEPP, 2015. As of August 30, 2017: https://www.rand.org/pubs/research_reports/RR1118.html

Criminal Complaint, *U.S. v. Lepsky*, D.N.J., May 4, 2017 (Magistrate 17-8071). As of August 30, 2017: https://www.justice.gov/opa/press-release/file/964546/download

DHS—*See* U.S. Department of Homeland Security.

Economic and Social Research Council, "Prevent: UK's Counter Terrorism Strategy," undated. As of August 30, 2017: http://www.esrc.ac.uk/public-engagement/social-science-for-schools/resources/prevent-the-uk-s-counter-terrorism-strategy/

GfK NOP Social Research, *Attitudes to Living in Britain: Topline Findings*, April 27, 2006.

Green, Miranda, "Homeland Security Chief: Airplane Terror Threat 'Keeps Me Up at Night,'" CNN Politics, April 28, 2017. As of August 30, 2017: http://www.cnn.com/2017/04/28/politics/john-kelly-airplane-threats-cnntv/

Greenberg, Karen J., *Rogue Justice: The Making of the Security State*, New York: Crown Publishers, 2016a.

———, ed., *Case by Case: ISIS Prosecutions in the United States, March 1, 2014–June 30, 2016*, Center on National Security at Fordham Law, July 2016b. As of August 30, 2017: https://static1.squarespace.com/static/55dc76f7e4b013c872183fea/t/577c5b43197aea832bd486c0/1467767622315/ISIS+Report+-+Case+by+Case+-+July2016.pdf

Hennessy, Patrick, and Melissa Kite, "Poll Reveals 40pc of Muslims Want Sharia Law in UK," *Telegraph*, February 19, 2006. As of August 30, 2017: http://www.telegraph.co.uk/news/uknews/1510866/Poll-reveals-40pc-of-Muslims-want-sharia-law-in-UK.html

"Home and Away: DHS and the Threats to America, Remarks Delivered by Secretary Kelly at George Washington University Center for Cyber and Homeland Security," U.S. Department of Homeland Security, April 18, 2017. As of August 30, 2017: https://www.dhs.gov/news/2017/04/18/home-and-away-dhs-and-threats-america

Investigative Project on Terrorism, home page, undated (a). As of August 30, 2017: https://www.investigativeproject.org

———, *America's Refugee, Asylum, and Visa Waiver Programs: Our Entire Access System Is Broken*, undated (b). As of August 30, 2017: https://www.investigativeproject.org/documents/testimony/403.pdf

Jachimowicz, Maia, and Ramah McKay, "'Special Registration' Program," Migration Policy Institute, April 1, 2003. As of August 30, 2017: http://www.migrationpolicy.org/article/special-registration-program

Jenkins, Brian Michael, *Defining the Role of a National Commission on the Prevention of Violent Extremism and Homegrown Terrorism*, testimony before the U.S. House of Representatives Committee on Homeland Security Subcommittee on Intelligence, Information Sharing, and Terrorism Risk Assessment, June 14, 2007, Santa Monica, Calif.: RAND Corporation, CT-285, 2007. As of August 30, 2017: https://www.rand.org/pubs/testimonies/CT285.html

———, *Stray Dogs and Virtual Armies: Radicalization and Recruitment to Jihadist Terrorism in the United States Since 9/11*, Santa Monica, Calif.: RAND Corporation, OP-343-RC, 2011. As of August 30, 2017: https://www.rand.org/pubs/occasional_papers/OP343.html

———, "When Jihadis Come Marching Home," *Hill*, November 19, 2014. As of August 30, 2017: http://thehill.com/blogs/pundits-blog/defense/224597-when-jihadis-come-marching-home

Jenkins, Brian Michael, and Bruce R. Butterworth, *The Threat to Air and Ground Transportation Posed by Mentally Disordered Assailants*, San Jose, Calif.: Mineta Transportation Institute, March 2017. As of August 30, 2017: http://transweb.sjsu.edu/PDFs/research/threat-to-air-and-ground-transportation-by-mentally-disordered-assailants.pdf

Jenkins, Brian Michael, and Jean-François Clair, *Trains, Concert Halls, Airports, and Restaurants—All Soft Targets: What the Terrorist Campaign in France and Belgium Tells Us About the Future of Jihadist Terrorism in Europe*, San Jose, Calif.: Mineta Transportation Institute, Report WP 12-10, June 2016. As of August 30, 2017: http://transweb.sjsu.edu/project/1532.html

Jenkins, Brian Michael, and Joseph Trella, *Carnage Interrupted: An Analysis of Fifteen Terrorist Plots Against Public Surface Transportation*, San Jose, Calif.: Mineta Transportation Institute, April 2012. As of August 30, 2017: http://transweb.sjsu.edu/project/2979.html

Joscelyn, Thomas, "AQAP Leader Calls for 'Simple' Attacks in the West," *FDD's Long War Journal*, May 8, 2017. As of August 30, 2017: http://www.longwarjournal.org/archives/2017/05/aqap-leader-calls-for-simple-attacks-in-the-west.php

Kepel, Giles, and Antoine Jardin, *Terror in France: The Rise of Jihad in the West*, Princeton, N.J.: Princeton Studies in Muslim Politics, 2017.

Krogstad, Jens Manuel, and Jynnah Radford, "Key Facts About Refugees to the U.S.," *Fact Tank: News in the Numbers*, Pew Research Center, January 30, 2017. As of August 30, 2017: http://www.pewresearch.org/fact-tank/2017/01/30/key-facts-about-refugees-to-the-u-s/

Kurzman, Charles, *Muslim-American Involvement with Violent Extremism, 2016*, Chapel Hill, N.C.: Triangle Center on Terrorism and Homeland Security, January 26, 2017. As of August 30, 2017: https://sites.duke.edu/tcths/files/2017/01/Kurzman_Muslim-American_Involvement_in_Violent_Extremism_2016.pdf

Lipka, Michael, "Muslims and Islam: Key Findings in the U.S. and Around the World," *Fact Tank: News in the Numbers*, Pew Research Center, February 27, 2017.

McGurk, Brett, special presidential envoy for the Global Coalition to Counter ISIL, U.S. Department of State, "Update on Campaign Against ISIL," briefing, October 7, 2016. As of August 30, 2017: https://2009-2017.state.gov/r/pa/prs/ps/2016/10/262934.htm

Mueller, John, ed., *Terrorism Since 9/11: The American Cases*, Columbus, Ohio: Ohio State University, Mershon Center for International Security Studies, January 2017. As of August 30, 2017: http://politicalscience.osu.edu/faculty/jmueller/SINCE.pdf

Pew Research Center, *Muslim Americans: Middle Class and Mostly Mainstream—War on Terror Concerns*, Washington, D.C., May 22, 2007. As of August 30, 2017: http://www.people-press.org/2007/05/22/muslim-americans-middle-class-and-mostly-mainstream/

———, *Muslim Americans: No Signs of Growth in Alienation or Support for Extremism*, Washington, D.C., August 30, 2011. As of August 30, 2017: http://www.people-press.org/2011/08/30/muslim-americans-no-signs-of-growth-in-alienation-or-support-for-extremism/

Porter, Tom, "Isis Targeting Misfits and Mentally Ill to Commit Lone-Wolf Terror Attacks, Claims UK Police Chief," *International Business Times*, undated. As of August 30, 2017: http://www.ibtimes.co.uk/isis-targetting-misfits-mentally-ill-commit-lone-wolf-terror-attacks-claims-uk-police-chief-1497968

Possley, Maurice, "Ahmed Hannan," National Registry of Exonerations, undated. As of August 30, 2017: https://www.law.umich.edu/special/exoneration/Pages/casedetail.aspx?caseid=3275

Rasmussen, Nicholas J., director, National Counterterrorism Center, "Countering Violent Islamist Extremism: The Urgent Threat of Foreign Fighters and Homegrown Terror," testimony before the U.S. House of Representatives Committee on Homeland Security, February 11, 2015. As of August 30, 2017: http://docs.house.gov/meetings/HM/HM00/20150211/102901/HHRG-114-HM00-Wstate-RasmussenN-20150211.pdf

Salama, Vivian, and Alicia A. Caldwell, "AP Exclusive: DHS Report Disputes Threat from Banned Nations," Associated Press, February 24, 2017. As of August 30, 2017: https://apnews.com/39f1f8e4ceed4a30a4570f693291c866/dhs-intel-report-disputes-threat-posed-travel-ban-nations

Schneiderman, Eric T., attorney general, State of New York, letter to President Barack Obama urging the President to rescind the National Security Entry–Exit Registration System regulatory framework, December 19, 2016. As of August 30, 2017: https://ag.ny.gov/sites/default/files/nseers.pdf

UK Ministry of Justice, *Policy Paper: 2010 to 2015 Government Policy—Counter-Terrorism*, May 8, 2015. As of August 30, 2017: https://www.gov.uk/government/publications/2010-to-2015-government-policy-counter-terrorism/2010-to-2015-government-policy-counter-terrorism

U.S. Code, Title 18, Crimes and criminal procedure, Part I, Crimes, Chapter 113B, Terrorism, Section 2332A, Use of weapons of mass destruction. As of September 1, 2017: https://www.gpo.gov/fdsys/granule/USCODE-2011-title18/USCODE-2011-title18-partI-chap113B-sec2332a/content-detail.html

U.S. Code, Title 18, Crimes and criminal procedure, Part I, Crimes, Chapter 113B, Terrorism, Section 2339A, Providing material support to terrorists. As of September 1, 2017: https://www.gpo.gov/fdsys/granule/USCODE-2010-title18/USCODE-2010-title18-partI-chap113B-sec2339A

U.S. Code, Title 18, Crimes and criminal procedure, Part I, Crimes, Chapter 113B, Terrorism, Section 2339B, Providing material support or resources to designated foreign terrorist organizations. As of September 1, 2017: https://www.gpo.gov/fdsys/granule/USCODE-2010-title18/USCODE-2010-title18-partI-chap113B-sec2339B

U.S. Code, Title 18, Crimes and criminal procedure, Part I, Crimes, Chapter 113B, Terrorism, Section 2339C, Prohibitions against the financing of terrorism. As of September 1, 2017: https://www.gpo.gov/fdsys/granule/USCODE-2010-title18/USCODE-2010-title18-partI-chap113B-sec2339C

U.S. Department of Homeland Security, Acting Under Secretary for Intelligence and Analysis, "Citizenship Likely an Unreliable Indicator of Terrorist Threat to the United States," undated.

———, "Home and Away: DHS and the Threats to America, Remarks Delivered by Secretary Kelly at George Washington University Center for Cyber and Homeland Security," release date April 18, 2017. As of October 18, 2017: https://www.dhs.gov/news/2017/04/18/home-and-away-dhs-and-threats-america

———, "Yearbook of Immigration Statistics 2015," last published May 16, 2017b. As of August 30, 2017: https://www.dhs.gov/immigration-statistics/yearbook/2015

U.S. Department of Justice, Office of the Inspector General, *The September 11 Detainees: A Review of the Treatment of Aliens Held on Immigration Charges in Connection with the Investigation of the September 11 Attacks*, Washington, D.C., April 2003. As of August 30, 2017: https://oig.justice.gov/special/0306/full.pdf

U.S. House of Representatives Committee on Homeland Security, "Terror Threat Snapshot," undated. As of August 30, 2017: https://homeland.house.gov/map/

van Ginkel, Bibi, and Eva Entenmann, eds., *The Foreign Fighters Phenomenon in the European Union: Profiles, Threats and Policies*, The Hague: International Centre for Counter-Terrorism, April 2016. As of August 30, 2017: https://www.icct.nl/wp-content/uploads/2016/03/ICCT-Report_Foreign-Fighters-Phenomenon-in-the-EU_1-April-2016_including-AnnexesLinks.pdf

Vidino, Lorenzo, and Seamus Hughes, *Countering Violent Extremism in America*, Washington, D.C.: Center for Cyber and Homeland Security, George Washington University, June 2015a. As of August 30, 2017: https://cchs.gwu.edu/sites/cchs.gwu.edu/files/downloads/CVE%20in%20America%20.pdf

———, *ISIS in America: From Retweets to Raqqa*, Washington, D.C.: George Washington University Program on Extremism, December 2015b. As of August 30, 2017: https://cchs.gwu.edu/sites/cchs.gwu.edu/files/downloads/ISIS%20in%20America%20-%20Full%20Report.pdf

Walters, Riley, "An Interactive Timeline of the 85 Islamist Terror Plots Since 9/11," *Daily Signal*, May 16, 2016. As of August 30, 2017: http://dailysignal.com/2016/05/16/an-interactive-timeline-of-the-85-islamist-terror-plots-since-911/

Weiner, Rachel, "20-Year-Old Says He Planned ISIS Terror Attacks in Virginia, North Carolina," *Washington Post*, November 29, 2016.

White House, *Empowering Local Partners to Prevent Violent Extremism in the United States*, Washington, D.C., August 2011. As of August 30, 2017: https://obamawhitehouse.archives.gov/sites/default/files/empowering_local_partners.pdf

———, "Fact Sheet: The White House Summit on Countering Violent Extremism," February 18, 2015a. As of August 30, 2017: https://obamawhitehouse.archives.gov/the-press-office/2015/02/18/fact-sheet-white-house-summit-countering-violent-extremism

———, "Remarks by the President at the Summit on Countering Violent Extremism," February 19, 2015b. As of August 30, 2017: https://obamawhitehouse.archives.gov/the-press-office/2015/02/19/remarks-president-summit-countering-violent-extremism-february-19-2015

Wike, Richard, and Greg Smith, "Little Support for Terrorism Among Muslim Americans," Washington, D.C.: Pew Research Center, December 17, 2009. As of August 30, 2017:
http://www.pewforum.org/2009/12/17/little-support-for-terrorism-among-muslim-americans/

The Chronology

Those with an asterisk (*) are actual attacks. The others are terrorist plots.

MAY 2002

Padilla terrorist plot. José Padilla, a U.S.-born convert to Islam, traveled to Afghanistan and joined al Qaeda sometime in 2001. He returned to the United States in 2002, allegedly to carry out terrorist attacks. He was held in military custody for five years; his trial did not commence until 2007. Several charges were dropped, but he was found guilty on the remaining counts.

Plot to bomb electrical substations in Florida. Imran Mandhai, a Pakistani immigrant, who had been on the FBI's radar since 2000, was arrested for plotting to bomb electrical substations in Florida. He and his codefendant also looked at other targets, including National Guard armories.

JULY 2002

***Shooting at Los Angeles International Airport.** Hesham Mohamed Hadayet, an Egyptian national still living in the United States after his request for asylum had been rejected, opened fire at the El Al check-in counter, killing two people and injuring four others, before he was shot and killed by El Al security guards. Federal authorities later concluded that the assault was a terrorist attack.

MARCH 2003

Plot to bomb underground fuel-storage tanks at gas stations in Maryland. Uzair Paracha was convicted of assisting Majid Khan, an al Qaeda operative, to enter the United States in order to bomb gas stations in Maryland.

Shukrijumah terrorist plots. Adnan Gulshair el Shukrijumah, born in Saudi Arabia, came to the United States as a young teenager with his parents. He might have trained with al Qaeda in Afghanistan in the late 1990s and returned to the United States, where he came to the attention of the authorities in 2001, but he reportedly left the country in May of that year, although there were subsequent sightings of him in the United States. He was believed to be involved in several terrorist plots in the United States. A warrant for his arrest as a material witness was issued in March 2003. He was reported to have been killed in Pakistan in 2014.

MAY 2003	**Plot to destroy the Brooklyn Bridge.** Lyman Faris, a naturalized U.S. citizen from Kashmir with a history of mental problems, had traveled to Afghanistan in 2000, where he joined al Qaeda and then returned to the United States after several months. In 2002, he was involved in a plot to destroy the Brooklyn Bridge, which he abandoned as unrealistic. Detained in 2003, he was later convicted on terrorism charges.
JUNE 2003	**Plot to kill President George W. Bush** while overseas and launch a terrorist campaign in the United States. Ahmed Omar Abu Ali, a U.S.-born citizen and a member of al Qaeda, was arrested by Saudi authorities and extradited to the United States, where he was tried and convicted.
	Virginia "Jihad Network." The group, which was connected with the Pakistani jihadist group Lashkar-e-Taiba, trained to carry out unspecified attacks against U.S. forces in Afghanistan. Prosecutors presented no evidence that the defendants planned specific attacks in the United States but claimed that had the group planned to wage war on all countries deemed enemies of Islam. Ultimately, 12 men were convicted.
SEPTEMBER 2003	**Alamoudi plot to assassinate then–Saudi Prince Abdullah.** Abdurahman Alamoudi, a naturalized U.S. citizen, was arrested in 2003 for involvement in a Libyan-backed plot to assassinate Saudi Crown Prince Abdullah. He was convicted in 2004.
NOVEMBER 2003	**Plot to bomb a shopping mall in Columbus, Ohio.** Nuradin Abdi, a Somali refugee who arrived in the United States in 1999, initiated a plot to blow up a shopping mall in Columbus, Ohio. He was an associate of Lyman Faris (see May 2003 plot to destroy the Brooklyn Bridge) and Christopher Paul (see June 2008 plot below).

AUGUST 2004

Plot to blow up a federal courthouse in Chicago. Angry at the federal government, Gale Nettles acquired a large amount of what he believed to be ammonium nitrate from an FBI undercover agent, paying for it with counterfeit bills, which he had manufactured. He then sought to sell the explosives to al Qaeda or another terrorist group, in fact represented by another undercover agent, suggesting that the group could use the explosives to bomb the courthouse in Chicago.

Plot to attack financial institutions in New York. Dhiren Barot was born in India but moved to the UK when he was one. He converted to Islam when he was 20. In the 1990s, he spent time in Pakistan engaged in actions against Indian forces in Kashmir. He later became an al Qaeda operative. He arrived in the United States in 2000, where he began reconnoitering financial institutions for a possible bombing. He returned to the UK, where he also plotted terrorist attacks on hotels, the London Tube, and railway stations. These terrorist projects were proposed for al Qaeda funding. While he was in the UK, his plans came to the attention of both U.S. and UK authorities. Along with seven other men, he was arrested in 2004 and convicted of terrorist plotting.

Plot to bomb a New York City subway station during the Republican National Convention. Two men were arrested for plotting to carry out a bombing of a subway station near Madison Square Garden in New York City, where the Republican National Convention was to take place.

Aref terrorist plot. Two men (Yassin M. Aref and Mohammed M. Hossain) were arrested for plotting to assassinate a Pakistani diplomat in the United States with a shoulder-fired missile to be provided by an FBI undercover agent.

OCTOBER 2004

Ahmed Hassan Al-Uqaily case. Federal authorities in Tennessee arrested Ahmed Hassan Al-Uqaily after he took possession of two machine guns and four hand grenades provided to him as part of an undercover investigation. Angered at U.S. policy in Iraq, Al-Uqaily, who said he was "going jihad" and planned to "blow up something," began to amass a small arsenal. He hoped to acquire an antitank missile, as well as machine guns and grenades. He did not identify any specific target.

MARCH 2005 **Plot to build a bomb for a terrorist attack in the United States.** While in prison in Malta awaiting extradition to the United States for kidnapping his two children in a custody battle, Ronald Grecula offered to build a bomb and sell it to al Qaeda or any such group for a terrorist attack in the United States.

JUNE 2005 **Lodi terrorist plot.** Hamid Hayat, who spent nearly two years at an al Qaeda training camp in Afghanistan, was arrested after his return to the United States. Federal prosecutors claimed that he was sent back to conduct terrorist attacks in the United States, although he was charged and convicted of providing material support and making false statements to federal investigators. Hamid's father, Umer Hayat, was also convicted of lying to investigators. His trial ended in a hung jury, but he subsequently pleaded guilty in return for a sentence of time served.

AUGUST 2005 **Plot to attack National Guard facilities and synagogues** in southern California (also called the "Los Angeles bomb plot"). During a routine investigation of a series of armed robberies at gas stations in southern California, local police discovered that the purpose of the robberies was to fund a terrorist campaign planned in prison. Although no bombs had been built or specific targets chosen, the four men involved, one of whom was still in prison, intended to attack National Guard armories and synagogues.

DECEMBER 2005 **Offer to blow up a Montana refinery and oil and gas pipelines.** Michael Curtis Reynolds was arrested for planning to blow up a refinery, the Alaska pipeline, and other pipelines.

FEBRUARY 2006 **Toledo terror cell.** Although this well-known case was clearly a homegrown terrorist plot that included efforts to recruit others in the United States, the three men involved were indicted on charges of plotting to kill Americans overseas, making the case a questionable inclusion.

MARCH 2006 ***Car ramming at University of North Carolina.** Mohammed Reza Taheri-azar, a naturalized U.S. citizen who had come to the United States from Iran when he was two, rammed a rented vehicle into a group of fellow students at the University of North Carolina, injuring nine people, none seriously. He proclaimed to be an admirer of Mohamed Atta, the leader of the 9/11 hijackers, and said that he wanted to avenge the murder of Muslims around the world.

APRIL 2006

Plot to attack targets in Washington, D.C. Two people were arrested in Atlanta for conducting reconnaissance missions of possible targets of terrorist operations in Washington, D.C., including the U.S. Capitol and the World Bank. One of the two had earlier attempted to join Lashkar-e-Taiba.

JUNE 2006

Plot to bomb the Sears Tower in Chicago (sometimes referred to as the "Liberty City Seven" case). Seven men in Florida were charged with planning terrorist attacks on targets in the United States, including what was then called the Sears Tower in Chicago and federal buildings in Florida. Although an informant who posed as an al Qaeda agent offered the group money in return for carrying out attacks, the conspirators were not Muslims but members of a local cult that combined beliefs in Judaism and Christianity with bits of Islam and voodoo. After two mistrials resulting from hung juries, five were ultimately convicted and two were acquitted. Four of those convicted were U.S.-born citizens; the fifth was a Haitian national.

DECEMBER 2006

Plot to bomb a shopping mall in Rockford, Illinois. Derrick Shareef, a U.S.-born convert to Islam, was arrested for plotting to set off grenades at a local shopping mall just before Christmas.

MAY 2007

Plot to attack soldiers at Fort Dix, New Jersey. Six men were arrested for plotting to attack and kill as many soldiers as possible at Fort Dix, New Jersey.

JUNE 2007

Plot to attack facilities at JFK International Airport in New York. Russell Defreitas, a naturalized U.S. citizen from Guyana, was arrested as the leader of a plot to bomb aviation fuel pipelines at JFK International Airport in New York. Three others, all foreign nationals (two citizens of Guyana and one of Trinidad and Tobago), participated in the plot. They were later extradited to the United States and convicted along with Defreitas of conspiracy to cause death and destruction.

JUNE 2008

Christopher Paul plot. Christopher Paul, a U.S.-born convert to Islam, had joined al Qaeda in Afghanistan in 1990 and reportedly fought in Bosnia. He returned to the United States but, in 1999, became connected with a terrorist cell in Germany. Returning to his home in Ohio, he became acquainted with both Lyman Faris (see May 2003 plot to destroy the Brooklyn Bridge) and Nuradin Abdi (see November 2003 plot to bomb a shopping mall in Columbus, Ohio). Paul was convicted of planning to carry out terrorist attacks in the United States and abroad.

JUNE 2008–JANUARY 2009

Vinas plot to attack the Long Island Rail Road. In 2007, Bryant Neal Vinas, a U.S.-born citizen and convert to Islam, traveled to Pakistan, where he joined al Qaeda. He participated in operations against U.S. forces in Afghanistan but was approached by al Qaeda planners to be trained in explosives and participate in a terrorist attack on the Long Island Rail Road. Vinas, however, was captured by Pakistani forces and sent to the United States, where he was tried as a terrorist. In custody, Vinas cooperated with authorities and became an extremely valuable source in assisting them in thwarting other terrorist plots and prosecuting other terrorists. As a consequence, after spending eight years in solitary confinement, he was sentenced to eight years, including time served, and was scheduled to be released later in 2017.

MAY 2009

Plot to bomb synagogue in Bronx, New York. Four men (three U.S.-born citizens and a Haitian immigrant) were arrested for plotting to blow up two synagogues in the Riverdale neighborhood of Bronx, New York, as well as shoot down military planes flying out of Stewart Air National Guard Base in nearby Newburgh, New York.

JUNE 2009

***Little Rock shooting.** In a drive-by shooting at military recruiting office in Little Rock, Arkansas, Carlos Bledsoe, a U.S.-born convert to Islam, killed one soldier and wounded another. Bledsoe previously had spent 16 months in Yemen teaching English but was arrested while there for overstaying his visa and deported back to the United States. While awaiting trial on terrorism charges, Bledsoe claimed that he was a soldier of al Qaeda, but this was never confirmed and might simply have been an attempt at self-aggrandizement. He was convicted of murder in state court rather than on federal charges.

JULY 2009

North Carolina cluster (or Raleigh jihad group). Seven men were arrested in North Carolina for conspiring to carry out terrorist attacks abroad; however, two members of the group were also indicted for plotting to attack military personnel at the Marine Corps training base in Quantico, Virginia. An eighth conspirator, who had earlier fled to Pakistan, was indicted but not arrested. Five of the eight were U.S.-born citizens, two were naturalized U.S. citizens, and one was a legal permanent resident from Kosovo.

SEPTEMBER 2009

Plot to carry out suicide bombings on the New York subway. Najibullah Zazi, a legal permanent resident originally from Afghanistan, and two others plotters traveled to Afghanistan, where they were recruited and trained for a suicide attack on the New York subway. Zazi's father and a local imam were also convicted for lying to authorities during the investigation.

Plot to bomb a high-rise building in Dallas, Texas. Hosam Smadi, a Jordanian national, came to the United States in 2007 on a tourist visa, which he overstayed. Noting his increasingly violent rhetoric on the Internet, in which he said he wanted to imitate 9/11 and bring down a skyscraper, the FBI created a "sleeper cell" consisting of three FBI undercover agents, which ultimately met with and provided Smadi with a fake bomb. Although Smadi claimed loyalty to Osama bin Laden, he was not affiliated with any group, and FBI officials believed that he self-radicalized via the Internet.

Plot to bomb a federal courthouse in Springfield, Illinois. Michael Finton, a U.S.-born citizen who converted to Islam while in prison for armed robbery, was arrested by an FBI undercover agent for plotting to blow up a federal building.

OCTOBER 2009

Mehanna-Abousamra terrorist plot. Tarek Mehanna, a U.S.-born citizen, was arrested for plotting to support terrorists by seeking training from Islamic fighters overseas. Tarek's coconspirator was Ahmad Abousamra, a naturalized U.S. citizen from France, but he had departed for Syria in 2006 and never returned. According to the FBI, the two men had discussed randomly shooting people at a shopping mall and assassinating U.S. officials.

NOVEMBER 2009

***Fort Hood shooting.** Angry at U.S. policy and his anticipated deployment to Afghanistan, Nidal Hasan, a psychiatrist and major in the Army, opened fire on soldiers at Fort Hood, Texas, killing 13 and wounding more than 30 others. The case provoked a debate as to whether Hasan's motives were personal or ideological. Most labeled the attack an act of terrorism. This was irrelevant to Hasan's court-martial, which convicted him on 13 counts of murder and 32 counts of attempted murder.

MARCH 2010 **Chicago stadium bomb plot.** Raja Lahrasib Khan, a naturalized citizen from Pakistan, was arrested for sending funds to al Qaeda. The indictment, however, also describes conversations that Khan had in which he discussed planting remotely detonated bombs at a sports stadium in Chicago.

APRIL 2010 **Plot to bomb the New York Stock Exchange.** It is not clear that there was, in fact, a plot. Wesam El-Hanafi, a U.S.-born citizen; Sabirhan Hasanoff, a dual naturalized U.S. and Australian citizen who was born in China; and Khalid Ouazzani, a naturalized U.S. citizen from Morocco, were arrested for providing support to al Qaeda. All three at one time wanted to join al Qaeda, but, to prove their bona fides, they were asked to send money, which they did, and to conduct provide intelligence about potential targets for future terrorist attacks. Hasanoff specifically was asked to reconnoiter the New York Stock Exchange, and he produced a one-page report. The three Americans never indicated any willingness to engage in domestic terrorist attacks; they did not participate in any such planning; and they were not charged with any terrorist plot, although they remained determined to join al Qaeda abroad. Instead, the three were convicted of providing material support to a terrorist organization.[73]

MAY 2010 ***Times Square bombing.** Faisal Shahzad, a naturalized U.S. citizen of Pakistani descent, arrived to study in the United States in 1997. He was granted permanent residency status in 2006 and became a citizen in 2009, but he was also becoming increasingly radicalized. Later in 2009, he traveled to Pakistan, where he received explosives training. He returned to the United States and began to construct a car bomb—in fact, a large incendiary device—that he attempted to detonate in New York's Times Square. The device caught fire but failed to explode.

Rockwood assassination plot. Paul Rockwood, Jr., a U.S.-born convert to Islam angered by the U.S. war on terrorism, was arrested for compiling a hit list of possible targets for assassination. However, he was convicted of lying to federal investigators. His wife, a UK national, was also convicted but was deported to the UK, where she was allowed to serve her sentence on probation.

OCTOBER 2010 **Plot to bomb Washington, D.C., Metro.** Farooque Ahmed, a naturalized U.S. citizen who arrived from Pakistan as a teenager 17 years before, was arrested for plotting to bomb Metro stations near the Pentagon.

NOVEMBER 2010	**Plot to bomb a Christmas ceremony in Portland, Oregon.** Mohamed Osman Mohamud, a naturalized U.S. citizen from Somalia who arrived in the United States when he was four years old, detonated what he believed to be a vehicle bomb at a Christmas tree–lighting ceremony in Portland. In fact, the bomb was a fake device that FBI undercover agents provided to him, but his willingness to use it demonstrated intentions to carry out a terrorist attack.
DECEMBER 2010	**Plot to bomb a Baltimore, Maryland, recruiting center.** Antonio Martinez, a naturalized U.S. citizen from Nicaragua and convert to Islam, detonated what he believed to be a vehicle bomb at an armed forces recruiting center. The fake device had been provided by FBI undercover agents.
JANUARY 2011	**Emerson Begolly case.** As a teenager, Emerson Begolly, a U.S.-born citizen, espoused Nazi sympathies but later converted to Islam, becoming a prominent figure on jihadist website. Although he did not articulate any specific terrorist plot, he exhorted others to attack police stations, post offices, Jewish schools and daycare centers, military facilities, train lines, bridges, cell phone towers, and waterworks.
FEBRUARY 2011	**Khalid Aldawsari bombing plot.** Khalid Aldawsari, a Saudi national in the United States on a student visa, began to acquire chemicals for manufacturing explosives to be used in bombs for terrorist attacks. He had no specific plan when arrested but had contemplated attacking Americans who had been stationed at Abu Ghraib Prison in Iraq, reservoirs and hydroelectric dams, nuclear power plants, and the Dallas residence of former President George W. Bush. He also thought about detonating explosives-filled rental cars on crowded streets during rush hour in New York.
FEBRUARY–MAY 2011	**Ferhani plot to bomb a New York City synagogue.** Ahmed Ferhani, a legal permanent resident, and Mohamed Mamdouh, a naturalized U.S. citizen, both of whom had criminal records, were arrested by undercover officers while purchasing weapons for a planned assault on an unspecified New York synagogue, preferably the largest one in the city. Both were convicted on state rather than federal charges.

JUNE 2011	*Shots fired at the Pentagon.** Yonathan Melaku, a naturalized U.S. citizen from Ethiopia and convert to Islam, was arrested for a series of shootings at the Pentagon and other military facilities in the area, all of which occurred in October and November 2010.
	Plot to attack a Seattle recruiting center. Two men, both U.S.-born converts to Islam, were arrested for planning an armed assault at a military recruit processing station in Seattle.
JULY 2011	**Kodirov threat to assassinate President Obama.** Ulugbek Kodirov, who was in the United States on a revoked student visa, acting under instructions from a person he believed to be connected with the Islamic Movement of Uzbekistan, a designated foreign terrorist organization, initiated plans to kill President Obama. He was arrested attempting to acquire weapons and explosives from an FBI undercover agent.
	Planned a Fort Hood–style attack. After Private First Class Naser Jason Abdo objected, as a Muslim, to his deployment to Afghanistan, the Army agreed to discharge the U.S.-born citizen but then discovered child pornography on his computer. Facing a court-martial, Abdo went absent without leave from Fort Campbell, Kentucky. He plotted to carry out a Fort Hood–style attack by setting off a bomb at a restaurant where soldiers from Fort Hood frequently ate, then shooting survivors as they fled.
JULY–SEPTEMBER 2011	**Plot to attack government buildings** with remote-controlled model airplanes. Rezwan Ferdaus, a U.S.-born citizen, was arrested for plotting to pack model airplanes with explosives and fly them into the Pentagon, the U.S. Capitol, and other government buildings.
NOVEMBER 2011	**Pimentel plot to attack returning U.S. service personnel.** José Pimentel, a naturalized U.S. citizen from the Dominican Republic, plotted to make pipe bombs, using match heads, and use them to attack U.S. service personnel returning from Afghanistan and Iraq, as well as other targets.
NOVEMBER 2011–JANUARY 2012	**Osmakac plot to attack targets in Florida.** Sami Osmakac, a naturalized U.S. citizen from Kosovo, planned to set off car bombs, carry out armed attacks, and seize hostages to make unspecified demands. His list of targets included nightclubs, police stations, six bridges connecting Tampa to the mainland, and other businesses, including a Starbucks coffee shop. He aroused suspicion when he went to a local shop to buy an al Qaeda flag.

FEBRUARY 2012	**Planned suicide bombing of the U.S. Capitol.** Amine El Khalifi, who came from Morocco on a visitor's visa at the age of 16 but continued to live in the United States illegally after his visa expired, was arrested in an FBI undercover operation for plotting to carry out a suicide bombing at the Capitol building in Washington.
FEBRUARY–OCTOBER 2012	**Plot to blow up the U.S. Federal Reserve building in New York.** Quazi Nafis, a Bangladeshi national in the United States on a student visa, plotted with FBI undercover agents to blow up the Federal Reserve building in New York with what he believed to be a car bomb that the FBI provided to him.
NOVEMBER 2012	**Qazi brothers' bomb plot.** Sheheryar Qazi and Raees Alam Qazi, two brothers from Pakistan and both naturalized citizens, planned to blow up targets in New York City in order to avenge U.S. drone strikes. Raees traveled to New York to reconnoiter possible targets, including Wall Street, Times Square, and nearby theaters.

FEBRUARY 2013	**Erwin Antonio Rios robbery and murder plot.** Needing funds to travel overseas to join jihadists in Syria, Erwin Antonio Rios, a U.S.-born convert to Islam, planned to carry out a series of armed robberies, leaving no surviving witnesses. He acquired a weapon from a confidential informant working for the FBI. This led to his arrest and conviction for possession of a stolen firearm.
	Plot to blow up an Oakland, California, bank on behalf of the Taliban. Matthew Aaron Llaneza, a U.S.-born citizen and convert to Islam who had once tried to join the Marine Corps, attempted to detonate what he believed was a vehicle bomb in front of a bank in Oakland, California. He hoped that the explosion would be blamed on antigovernment militias and trigger a civil war.
APRIL 2013	***Boston Marathon bombing.** Tamerlan Tsarnaev, an asylum seeker from Russia, and his younger brother Dzhokhar, a naturalized U.S. citizen, radicalized themselves and, using instructions available on the Internet, built two pressure-cooker bombs, which they detonated at the finish line of the Boston Marathon. Three persons were killed in the explosions, and several hundred were injured. The escaping bombers killed one person and wounded another (who died of his injuries months later) during their attempted escape.

MAY 2013

Kurbanov bomb plot. Fazliddin Kurbanov, a refugee from Uzbekistan, was arrested in Boise, Idaho, for supporting the Islamic Movement of Uzbekistan, a designated foreign terrorist organization; possessing bombs; and providing instructions on building bombs to be used in attacks on public transportation facilities and infrastructure targets. Prosecutors did not specify whether the bombs were to be used in the United States or abroad.

DECEMBER 2013

Wichita Dwight D. Eisenhower National Airport bomb plot. Terry Lee Loewen, a U.S.-born convert to Islam who radicalized himself on the Internet and who was an airport employee, made an offer to FBI undercover agents whom he believed were connected with al Qaeda in the Arabian Peninsula. He offered to detonate a vehicle bomb at the airport that he hoped would cause maximum casualties. The FBI had provided him with a vehicle and a fake bomb. He was arrested as he attempted to access the airport.

AUGUST 2014

***Ali Brown murders.** Authorities charged Ali Muhammad Brown, a U.S.-born citizen, convicted sex offender, and convert to Islam. He was found guilty on state charges of four counts of murder in Washington State and New Jersey. Although some of the murders were committed in the course of armed robberies, Brown, who was on the FBI's terrorist watch list, claimed that the killings were justified retribution for U.S. actions in Afghanistan, Iraq, and Syria. In 2016, Brown was sentenced to 36 years in prison. He faces additional penalties for three of the murders in Washington State.

SEPTEMBER 2014

***Oklahoma City beheading.** Alton Nolen, a U.S.-born citizen and recent convert to Islam, attacked two employees at a food processing plant from which he had just been fired. He slashed the throat of one woman, beheaded her, and stabbed a second and tried to behead her before he was shot and wounded. The inclusion of this attack is problematic. Some lists include it as an act of terrorism, while others do not. Although Nolen reportedly shouted something in Arabic during the attack, it is not clear whether the attack was motivated by ideology or personal reasons. He apparently had some fascination with photos of recent terrorist beheadings. Nolen was judged mentally incompetent to stand trial and was sent to a state mental hospital. However, he was subsequently judged competent to stand trial.

Elfgeeh murder plot. Mufid Elfgeeh, a naturalized U.S. citizen from Yemen who arrived in the United States when he was 13 years old, planned to murder active and former U.S. service personnel returning from Iraq. He also assisted others in traveling to Syria to join ISIS.

OCTOBER 2014

***Hatchet attack on New York City police officers.** Zale Thompson, a U.S.-born recent convert to Islam with a history of violence, attacked a group of four New York City Police Department officers with a metal hatchet. He wounded two of them before the other officers fatally shot him.

JANUARY 2015

Plot to bomb the Capitol building and assassinate U.S. officials. Christopher Cornell, a U.S.-born citizen and convert to Islam, planned to set off a bomb at the Capitol building and assassinate the President. He was sentenced to 30 years in prison.

Miguel Diaz plot. Miguel Moran Diaz, a Cuban-born immigrant who never became a U.S. citizen, was also a convicted felon and convert to Islam who described himself as a "lone wolf for ISIS." Doing so would show his allegiance to—and secure his membership in—ISIS. Diaz sought to acquire additional weapons for his small arsenal. His plan was to create panic by carrying out random sniper attacks, using shell casings with ISIS scratched on the shell casings, which the authorities would find.

FEBRUARY 2015

Plot to kill soldiers in North Carolina. Authorities arrested Zakaryia Abdin for plotting to kill U.S. soldiers at a military base near Raleigh, North Carolina. He was convicted as a juvenile and solely on a weapon charge. As a consequence, despite objections from law enforcement, he was paroled a year later in May 2016. In April 2017, he was arrested again at the Charleston International Airport as he attempted to board a plane to join ISIS. In a message sent to an undercover agent whom Abdin believed to be an ISIS operative, he requested that a hostage be reserved for him so that he could personally torture or execute a hostage and send a message to Americans.

MARCH 2015

Plot to attack National Guard soldiers in Illinois. Hasan and Jonas Edmonds, both U.S.-born converts to Islam who also were cousins, plotted to carry out a Fort Hood–like attack, aiming to kill as many as 150 National Guard soldiers at a Joliet, Illinois, armory. The third member of their assault team, however, was an FBI informant, and the two were arrested.

APRIL 2015

New York bomb-making plot. Noelle Velentzas, a U.S.-born convert to Islam, and Asia Siddiqui, a naturalized U.S. citizen from Saudi Arabia, were indicted for researching the fabrication of bombs they planned to use against targets in the United States.

Threats to U.S. officials. Mahamed Abukar Said, whose family immigrated to the United States from Ethiopia when he was one year old, was arrested for tweeting threats to kill the U.S. Attorney General and FBI officials following the arrest of four others for trying to join ISIS. There was no actual plot in this case.

Plot to carry out a suicide bombing at Fort Riley, Kansas. FBI agents arrested John T. Booker, Jr., a U.S.-born convert to Islam, for attempting to carry out a suicide bombing at Fort Riley, Kansas. The bomb was, in fact, a fake device provided by the FBI as part of an undercover operation. Booker had enlisted in the Army in 2014 solely for the purpose of carrying an attack like that at Fort Hood in 2009, but he was discharged before shipping out to basic training when the Army learned about comments he made on social media that he was prepared to die for jihad. That did not deter him from continuing to plot another attack, this time with a bomb. The FBI also arrested Alexander Blair, also a U.S.-born convert, for having knowledge of the plot, including lending money to Booker to purchase explosives, and for failing to notify the authorities.

MAY 2015

Munir Abdelkader terrorist plots. Munir Abdulkader is a naturalized citizen from Eritrea whose family came to the United States sometime before he was 11 years old. Acting at the urging of an ISIS operative with whom he was in touch on the Internet, Abdulkader planned to attack a police station and kill military service personnel. He was arrested three days after he acquired an AK-47.

***Garland, Texas, shooting.** Two roommates, both U.S.-born citizens, one a convert to Islam and the other the son of Pakistani parents, opened fire on security guards posted outside an art exhibit featuring cartoons of the prophet Muhammad. They wounded one guard but were fatally shot by police. A third man, also a U.S.-born convert, was later arrested for being part of the plot. He had been on the FBI's radar in connection with an earlier investigation of a plot to bomb the National Football League's Super Bowl in Phoenix.

JUNE 2015

Boston beheading plot. Usaamah Rahim, a U.S.-born citizen, plotted with his nephew, David Wright, a U.S.-born convert to Islam, to behead a well-known activist widely regarded as anti-Muslim. Deciding that was too difficult, he decided to behead a police officer instead. However, the FBI already had Rahim under surveillance. When police and federal agents attempted to arrest him, he reportedly tried to attack them with a knife and was shot. Wright and Nicholas Rovinski, a U.S.-born convert to Islam and allegedly a third conspirator, were arrested and later pleaded guilty to a charge of supporting a terrorist organization.

Mass killing plot in Virginia and North Carolina. Justin Sullivan, a U.S.-born convert to Islam, began plotting to carry out mass shootings at bars, concerts, and other public places on behalf of ISIS, which he contacted on the Internet. He also is accused of murdering an elderly neighbor.

Munther Omar Saleh bomb plot. Acting on instructions from ISIS, Munther Omar Saleh, a U.S. citizen, and Fareed Mumuni, a naturalized U.S. citizen, plotted to build a pressure-cooker bomb. They discussed targeting New York's Times Square and One World Trade Center. Mumuni stabbed an FBI agent during his arrest. A third defendant, Imran Rabbani, was charged with obstructing the investigation and sentenced to 20 months.

JULY 2015

Key West bombing plot. FBI agents arrested Harlem Suarez, a legal permanent resident from Cuba and convert to Islam, for plotting to carry out a bombing on behalf of ISIS. His targets included Independence Day crowds at a public beach in Key West, Marathon, or Miami.

***Chattanooga shooting.** Muhammad Youssef Abdulazeez, a naturalized U.S. citizen from Kuwait who arrived in the United States with his parents when he was six years old, opened fire at an armed forces recruiting center in Chattanooga. He then drove to a Navy Operational Support Center, where he fatally shot five service members before being killed by a police officer.

Alexander Ciccolo case. Alexander Ciccolo, a U.S.-born convert to Islam and the son of a police officer who warned the FBI that his son wanted to join ISIS, was arrested for plotting to bomb a university and broadcast executions of the students. Ciccolo acquired a small arsenal and instructions for making bombs. Ciccolo reportedly also had a long history of mental illness.

AUGUST 2015

Abdirahman Sheik Mohamud case. Following in his brother's footsteps, Abdirahman Sheik Mohamud, a Somali-born naturalized U.S. citizen, went to Syria to join al Qaeda's affiliate, Jabhat al-Nusra. Mohamud returned to the United States after his brother was killed, but he planned to obtain a weapon and conduct terrorist attacks against uniformed personnel (military or police). In June 2017, he pleaded guilty to providing support to a terrorist organization.

SEPTEMBER 2015

Plot to assassinate the pope. Santos Colon, Jr., a 15-year-old U.S. citizen, who sometimes used the name Ahmad Shakoor, sought to hire a sniper in a plot to assassinate the pope during his visit to the United States in September 2015. He also wanted to detonate a series of bombs in the surrounding area. Santos was previously a patient at a mental hospital.

NOVEMBER 2015

*__Merced campus stabbings.__ Faisal Mohammad, a U.S.-born citizen and student at the University of California Merced, stabbed and injured four people before he was fatally shot by university police.

Terrence McNeil case. Terrence McNeil, a U.S.-born convert to Islam, posted the names, photographs, and addresses of military service personnel and urged that they be killed. He did not have a specific plot to kill them himself.

NOVEMBER–DECEMBER 2015

*__San Bernardino shooting.__ Syed Farook, a U.S.-born citizen and Iraq War veteran, and his wife, Tashfeen Malik, a legal permanent resident, opened fire at an event where Farook worked. The two killed 14 people and wounded 22 others. Farook and Malik were later killed in a shootout with police. Enrique Marquez, Jr., a U.S.-born convert to Islam and former classmate and neighbor of Farook, was later arrested and convicted of providing the weapons used in the attack, although prosecutors also allege that he and Farook had previously discussed other terrorist attacks.

DECEMBER 2015

Mohamed Abdullahi Hassan case. Mohamed Abdullahi Hassan, a U.S. legal permanent resident of Somali origin, returned to Somalia and joined al Qaeda's affiliate, al Shabaab, in 2008. Considered to be the instigator of the May 2015 attack on the Muhammad cartoon exhibit in Garland, Texas, Hassan was also reportedly in touch with Syed Farook and Tashfeen Malik shortly before their attack in San Bernardino. Hassan surrendered to Somali authorities in December 2015.

ISIS funding to carry out a terrorist attack. Mohamed Yousef Elshinawy, a naturalized U.S. citizen from Egypt, received approximately $9,000 from ISIS to carry out a terrorist operation in the United States. No specific plot was elaborated, but the Garland, Texas, shooting was cited as an example.

Emanuel Lutchman plot. Emanuel Lutchman, a U.S.-born convert to Islam, acting at the urging of an ISIS contact overseas, planned to carry out a machete attack on diners at a Rochester, New York, restaurant. Theoretically, the plot involved another unidentified person. The attack would create panic and confusion, during which Lutchman and his partner would escape with a female hostage and take her back to his apartment, where they would video-record themselves beheading her.

JANUARY 2016

Houston shopping mall bomb plot. Omar Faraj Saeed al Hardan, a legal permanent resident who arrived in the United States as an Iraqi refugee in 2009, plotted to detonate a bomb at a Houston shopping mall. He also spoke about blowing up High Mobility Multipurpose Wheeled Vehicles (HMMWVs, commonly known as Humvees) at a nearby military base.

Plot to attack a Masonic temple. Samy Mohamed Hamzeh, a U.S.-born citizen, plotted to carry out a mass shooting at a Masonic temple in Milwaukee, Wisconsin.

***Attempted murder of a Philadelphia police officer.** In an attempt to murder a police officer, Edward Archer, a U.S.-born convert to Islam, opened fire on a police car he flagged down. Although wounded, the officer was able to wound Archer, who was arrested shortly afterward. Archer claimed that Allah ordered him to carry out the attack, but he was prosecuted on a state charge of attempted murder, rather than Pennsylvania's terrorism statute.

FEBRUARY 2016

Erick Jamal Hendricks case. Erick Jamal Hendricks, a U.S.-born convert to Islam, sought to recruit people via social media for a terrorist cell that would train together to carry out attacks in the United States on behalf of ISIS. There was no specific plot, although Hendricks identified military personnel and the woman who organized the "Draw Muhammad" contest in Texas as possible targets. Hendricks was in touch with one of the gunmen in the May 2015 Garland, Texas, attack on the exhibit. He is awaiting trial.

Plot to attack a Detroit church. Khalil Abu Rayyan, a U.S.-born citizen, acquired firearms, which he intended to use in attacks in the United States on behalf of ISIS. He mentioned a Detroit church and law enforcement personnel as targets he had considered. There was, however, no operational plan. He also said that he wanted to skin his victims "like sheep."

MAY 2016

Plot to bomb a Florida synagogue. James Gonzalo Medina, a U.S.-born convert to Islam, plotted to bomb a synagogue in Aventura, Florida. The FBI equipped him with a fake bomb and arrested him on his way to the target.

Threat to kill the President. While in jail on drug charges, Alex Hernandez, a U.S.-born convert to Islam, indicated in discussions with another inmate and later an undercover agent and in intercepted mail his desire to became a mujahid and kill the President of the United States.

JUNE 2016

***Orlando nightclub shooting.** Swearing allegiance to ISIS, Omar Mateen opened fire at an Orlando nightclub, killing 49 and wounding 53 others before he was killed by police. It was the worst mass shooting in U.S. history at the time. Seven months after the attack, Noor Salman, Mateen's wife, was charged with aiding Mateen's attack—prosecutors claim that she knew about the imminent attack and said nothing—and obstructing the subsequent investigation. As of this writing, she has pleaded not guilty.

JULY 2016

Sebastian Gregerson case. Sebastian Gregerson, a U.S.-born Muslim convert and reported supporter of ISIS, was arrested for acquiring hand grenades, which, investigators said, he planned to use in violent jihad. However, there was no specific terrorist plot and, as part of a deal with prosecutors, Gregerson pleaded guilty to explosives possession, which carries a maximum sentence of four years.

Plot to bomb targets in Arizona. FBI agents arrested Mahin Khan for plotting to carry out a terrorist attack in Arizona on behalf of ISIS. Possible targets included a Tucson synagogue, an office of the department of motor vehicles, and an Air Force Recruiting Office in Mesa, Arizona.

JULY 2016

Plot to carry out a Fort Hood–style shooting. Mohamed Bailor Jalloh, a naturalized U.S. citizen from Sierra Leone and former member of the Virginia Army National Guard, was recruited by ISIS during a visit to his homeland in 2015. After returning to the United States, Jalloh went back to Africa a second time in order to join ISIS in Libya, but then backed out. An ISIS contact put Jalloh in touch with an operative in the United States, where he would be able to assist him. That contact turned out to be an FBI informant with whom Jalloh discussed his new plans. These involved a Fort Hood–style attack on military personnel.

SEPTEMBER 2016

***Stabbings at St. Cloud shopping mall.** Dahir Adan, a naturalized U.S. citizen who had come to the United States as a refugee when he was two months old, began stabbing people at a shopping mall in Minnesota. He injured ten people. Although ISIS claimed responsibility for the attack, the FBI described it as a "potential" act of terrorism.

SEPTEMBER 2016

***Bombings in New Jersey and New York.** Ahmad Khan Rahami, a naturalized U.S. citizen who came to the United States from Afghanistan when he was 12 years old, planted three pipe bombs near the route of a local 5K run. Only one of the devices exploded. No one was injured. Later that day, a pressure-cooker bomb that Rahami made exploded in a sidewalk dumpster in Manhattan, injuring 31 people. Police later found a fifth unexploded device nearby.

OCTOBER 2016

Plot to kill a U.S. service member. Nelash Mohamed Das, a legal permanent resident from Bangladesh who entered the United States at the age of three, plotted on behalf of ISIS to kill a particular U.S. service member living nearby in Maryland. He got the name and address from an ISIS posting of U.S. military personnel to be killed. He reportedly thought that ISIS would pay him and his fellow conspirator (in fact, an FBI informant) $80,000 as a bounty for carrying out the operation.

Plot to bomb an Arizona prison. Thomas Orville Bastian, a U.S.-born convert to Islam who is serving a life sentence for murder, plotted to build and plant a bomb that would kill the warden or people in the visitors' area of the prison. Bastian's wife, Michelle, is accused of smuggling jihadist magazines containing bomb-making instructions into the prison in support of the scheme. According to some reports, Thomas Bastian became radicalized while in prison, but the plot might equally reflect personal motives.

NOVEMBER 2016

***Car ramming at Ohio State University.** Abdul Razak Ali Artan, a Somali refugee who was a legal permanent resident and a student at Ohio State University, rammed a car into a crowd of students at the university and then began stabbing people. In all, 13 people were injured in the attack. Artan was fatally shot by campus police.

JANUARY 2017

***Murder of a Denver security officer.** Joshua Cummings, a U.S.-born convert to Islam who, fellow worshippers had warned the FBI, was well advanced on the path to radicalization, fatally shot a Regional Transportation District security officer. Cummings had expressed strong antipolice sentiments in postings on the Internet and later said that he had pledged his loyalty to the head of ISIS.

FEBRUARY 2017

Plot to bomb transportation targets in Kansas City, Missouri. Robert Hester, a U.S.-born convert to Islam, plotted with undercover agents he believed to be ISIS operatives to carry out mass-casualty bombings targeting buses, trains, and a train station. Hester's FBI handler instructed Hester to acquire certain ingredients for making the bombs, which he did. He was then shown fake bombs, which would be hidden in backpacks.

Table 2. Plots and Attacks, 2002 to 2017

Education	<HS	did not complete secondary education
	HSG	completed high school or equivalent
	Some uni	earned some postsecondary credit
	BA/BS	completed four-year postsecondary program
	POST	completed some postbaccalaureate work
Status	INC	currently incarcerated
	REL	completed sentence and released
	DEC	deceased
	KILL	killed in the attack

Shaded rows show attacks.

Residency	U.S. born	born in the United States
	LPR	legal permanent resident
	NAT	naturalized citizen
	Asylum	granted asylum
	Student visa	on a student visa
	Illegal	in the United States illegally
	Refugee	refugee
	Visa unk	in the United States on an unknown visa
Groups	JEM	Jaish-e-Mohammed
	JIS	Jam'iyyat Ul-Islam Is-Saheeh
Abbreviations	SUV	sport-utility vehicle
	UNC Chapel Hill	University of North Carolina at Chapel Hill

Plot or Attack (attacks are highlighted)	Name	Gender	Year Born	Country of Origin	Year Entered the United States (if foreign born)	Age at Entry into the United States (if foreign born)	Years in the United States Before Arrest, Attack, or Death (if foreign born)
Plot against the United States generally	José Padilla	Male	1970	United States			
Plot to bomb Florida electrical substations	Imran Mandhai	Male	1983	Pakistan	1998	15	4
Plot to bomb Florida electrical substations	Shueyb Jokhan	Male	1978	Trinidad	1994	16	8
Hadayet attack on Los Angeles International Airport	Hesham Mohamed Hadayet	Male	1961	Egypt	1992	31	10
Plot to bomb Maryland gas stations	Uzair Paracha	Male	1980	Pakistan			
Plot to bomb Maryland gas stations	Saifullah Paracha	Male	1947	Pakistan			
Plot to bomb Maryland gas stations	Majid Khan	Male	1980	Pakistan	1996	16	7

Year of Plot or Attack	Age at Arrest or Attack	Name of Associated Group (if any)	Converted or Born into Islam	Residency	Education	Status	Note
2002	32	Al Qaeda	Convert	U.S. born	<HS	INC	
2002	19		Born	LPR	Some uni	REL	
2002	24		Born	NAT		REL	
2002	41		Born	LPR			
2003	23	Al Qaeda	Born	LPR	BA/BS	INC	
2003	56	Al Qaeda	Born	LPR	BA/BS	INC	
2003	23	Al Qaeda	Born	Asylum	HSG	INC	

Plot or Attack (attacks are highlighted)	Name	Gender	Year Born	Country of Origin	Year Entered the United States (if foreign born)	Age at Entry into the United States (if foreign born)	Years in the United States Before Arrest, Attack, or Death (if foreign born)
Plots against the New York City subway et al.	Adnan Gulshair el Shukrijumah	Male	1975	Saudi Arabia	1986	11	16
Plot against the Brooklyn Bridge	Lyman Faris	Male	1969	Kashmir	1994	25	9
Plot to kill President George W. Bush	Ahmed Omar Abu Ali	Male	1981	United States			
Virginia Jihad Network plots against U.S. targets in Afghanistan	Sabri Benkhala	Male	1976	United States			
Virginia Jihad Network plots against U.S. targets in Afghanistan	Randall Todd Royer	Male	1973	United States			
Virginia Jihad Network plots against U.S. targets in Afghanistan	Ibrahim al-Hamdi	Male	1978	Yemen	1993	15	10
Virginia Jihad Network plots against U.S. targets in Afghanistan	Khwaja Hasan	Male	1976	Pakistan			
Virginia Jihad Network plots against U.S. targets in Afghanistan	Muhammed Aatique	Male	1973	Pakistan	1996	23	7
Virginia Jihad Network plots against U.S. targets in Afghanistan	Donald Surratt	Male	1973	United States			
Virginia Jihad Network plots against U.S. targets in Afghanistan	Masoud Khan	Male	1972	Pakistan			
Virginia Jihad Network plots against U.S. targets in Afghanistan	Seifullah Chapman	Male	1973	United States			
Virginia Jihad Network plots against U.S. targets in Afghanistan	Hammad Abdur-Raheem	Male	1968	United States			
Virginia Jihad Network plots against U.S. targets in Afghanistan	Yong Kwon	Male	1976	South Korea			

Year of Plot or Attack	Age at Arrest or Attack	Name of Associated Group (if any)	Converted or Born into Islam	Residency	Education	Status	Note
2003	27	Al Qaeda	Born	LPR	Some uni	DEC	
2003	34	Al Qaeda	Born	NAT	<HS or HSG	INC	
2003	22	Al Qaeda	Born	U.S. born	Some uni	INC	
2003	27	Lashkar-e-Taiba	Born	U.S. born			
2003	30	Lashkar-e-Taiba	Convert	U.S. born	BA/BS	INC	
2003	25	Lashkar-e-Taiba	Born	LPR			
2003	27	Lashkar-e-Taiba	Born	NAT	POST		
2003	30	Lashkar-e-Taiba	Born	LPR	POST		
2003	30	Lashkar-e-Taiba	Convert	U.S. born		REL	
2003	31	Lashkar-e-Taiba	Born	NAT	POST	INC	
2003	30	Lashkar-e-Taiba	Convert	U.S. born	BA/BS	INC	
2003	35	Lashkar-e-Taiba	Convert	U.S. born	BA/BS		
2003	27	Lashkar-e-Taiba	Convert	NAT	BA/BS		

Plot or Attack (attacks are highlighted)	Name	Gender	Year Born	Country of Origin	Year Entered the United States (if foreign born)	Age at Entry into the United States (if foreign born)	Years in the United States Before Arrest, Attack, or Death (if foreign born)
Virginia Jihad Network plots against U.S. targets in Afghanistan	Ali al-Timimi	Male	1963	United States			
Virginia Jihad Network plots against U.S. targets in Afghanistan	Ali Chandia	Male	1976	Pakistan	1994	18	8
Plot to kill Saudi Prince Abdullah	Abdurahman Alamoudi	Male	1952	Eritrea	1979	27	24
Plot to bomb an Ohio shopping mall	Nuradin Abdi	Male	1972	Somalia	1998	26	6
Plot to sell bombing materials to a terrorist group	Gale Nettles	Male	1938	United States			
Plots to bomb New York City financial institutions	Dhiren Barot	Male	1972	India	2000	28	4
Plot to bomb a New York City subway station near the Republican Convention	Shahawar Siraj	Male	1982	Pakistan	1999	17	5
Plot to bomb a New York City subway station near the Republican Convention	James Elshafay	Male	1985	United States			
Plot to assassinate a Pakistani diplomat in the United States	Yassin M. Aref	Male	1970	Iraq	1999	29	5
Plot to assassinate a Pakistani diplomat in the United States	Mohammed M. Hossain	Male	1955	Bangladesh	1985	30	19
Plot to blow up an unknown U.S. target	Ahmed Hassan Al-Uqaily	Male	1971	Iraq			
Plot to build and sell a bomb to a group to use against the United States	Ronald Grecula	Male	1937	United States			
Plot to support terrorist groups	Umer Hayat	Male	1958	Pakistan			

Year of Plot or Attack	Age at Arrest or Attack	Name of Associated Group (if any)	Converted or Born into Islam	Residency	Education	Status	Note
2003	40	Lashkar-e-Taiba	Born	U.S. born	POST	INC	
2003	26	Lashkar-e-Taiba	Born	LPR	POST	INC	
2003	51	Al Qaeda, Hamas	Born	NAT		INC	
2003	32	Al Qaeda	Born	Asylum	Some uni		
2004	66			U.S. born		INC	
2004	32		Convert	Student visa			
2004	22		Born	Illegal		INC	
2004	19		Convert	U.S. born	HSG		
2004	34	JEM, Ansar al Islam	Born	Refugee	BA/BS	INC	
2004	49	JEM	Born	NAT	HSG	INC	
2004	33		Born	NAT		REL	
2005	68	Al Qaeda		U.S. born		REL	
2005	47	Al Qaeda, JEM	Born	NAT	<HS	REL	

Plot or Attack (attacks are highlighted)	Name	Gender	Year Born	Country of Origin	Year Entered the United States (if foreign born)	Age at Entry into the United States (if foreign born)	Years in the United States Before Arrest, Attack, or Death (if foreign born)
Plot to support terrorist groups	Hamid Hayat	Male	1982	United States			
Plot against Los Angeles targets	Kevin James	Male	1976	United States			
Plot against Los Angeles targets	Levar Washington	Male	1980	United States			
Plot against Los Angeles targets	Gregory Patterson	Male	1984	United States			
Plot against Los Angeles targets	Hammad Samana	Male	1984	Pakistan			
Plot to blow up an oil refinery and pipelines	Michael Curtis Reynolds	Male	1958	United States			
Plot to train insurgents against U.S. troops in Iraq	Mohammad Amawi	Male	1980	United States			
Plot to train insurgents against U.S. troops in Iraq	Marwan El-Hindi	Male	1963	Palestine	1984	21	22
Plot to train insurgents against U.S. troops in Iraq	Khaleel Ahmed	Male	1981	India			
Plot to train insurgents against U.S. troops in Iraq	Wassim Mazloum	Male	1981	Lebanon	2000	19	6
Plot to train insurgents against U.S. troops in Iraq	Zubair Ahmed	Male	1981	United States			
SUV attack against a crowd at UNC Chapel Hill	Mohammed Reza Taheri-azar	Male	1984	Iran	1985	2	20
Plot to attack D.C. targets	Syed Ahmed	Male	1984	Pakistan	1996	12	10
Plot to attack D.C. targets	Ehsanul Sadequee	Male	1986	United States			

Year of Plot or Attack	Age at Arrest or Attack	Name of Associated Group (if any)	Converted or Born into Islam	Residency	Education	Status	Note
2005	22	Al Qaeda, JEM	Born	U.S. born	<HS	INC	
2005	29	Self-established terrorist group (JIS)	Convert	U.S. born		INC	
2005	25	Self-established terrorist group (JIS)	Convert	U.S. born	<HS or HSG	INC	
2005	21	Self-established terrorist group (JIS)	Convert	U.S. born	Some uni		
2005	21	Self-established terrorist group (JIS)	Born	LPR	Some uni		
2005	47	Al Qaeda		U.S. born		INC	
2006	26		Born	U.S. born		INC	
2006	43		Born	NAT		INC	
2006	25		Born	NAT			
2006	25		Born	LPR			
2008	27		Born	U.S. born	Some uni		
2006	22		Born	NAT	BA/BS	INC	
2006	21	Al Qaeda, JEM, Lashkar-e-Taiba	Born	NAT	Some uni	INC	
2006	20	Al Qaeda, JEM, Lashkar-e-Taiba	Born	U.S. born	<HS	INC	

Plot or Attack (attacks are highlighted)	Name	Gender	Year Born	Country of Origin	Year Entered the United States (if foreign born)	Age at Entry into the United States (if foreign born)	Years in the United States Before Arrest, Attack, or Death (if foreign born)
Liberty City Seven plot to bomb the Sears Tower in Chicago	Narseal Batiste	Male	1974	United States			
Liberty City Seven plot to bomb the Sears Tower in Chicago	Burson Augustin	Male	1985	United States			
Liberty City Seven plot to bomb the Sears Tower in Chicago	Rothschild Augustin	Male	1983	United States			
Liberty City Seven plot to bomb the Sears Tower in Chicago	Stanley Phanor	Male	1975	United States			
Liberty City Seven plot to bomb the Sears Tower in Chicago	Patrick Abraham	Male	1979	Haiti	1997	18	9
Plot to use grenades against a Rockford, Illinois, shopping mall	Derrick Shareef	Male	1984	United States			
Fort Dix Five plot against military personnel at Fort Dix	Mohamad Shnewer	Male	1985	Jordan	1987	2	20
Fort Dix Five plot against military personnel at Fort Dix	Serdar Tatar	Male	1984	Turkey	1998	14	9
Fort Dix Five plot against military personnel at Fort Dix	Agron Abdullahu	Male	1983	Kosovo[a]	1999	16	8
Fort Dix Five plot against military personnel at Fort Dix	Dritan Duka	Male	1979	Albania	1984	5	23
Fort Dix Five plot against military personnel at Fort Dix	Shain Duka	Male	1981	Albania	1984	3	23
Fort Dix Five plot against military personnel at Fort Dix	Eljvir Duka	Male	1984	Albania	1984	0	23
Plot to bomb fuel pipelines at JFK International Airport	Russell Defreitas	Male	1944	Guyana			

[a]At the time of the plot, Kosovo was a part of Yugoslavia.

Year of Plot or Attack	Age at Arrest or Attack	Name of Associated Group (if any)	Converted or Born into Islam	Residency	Education	Status	Note
2006	32	Al Qaeda	Convert	U.S. born	HSG	INC	
2006	21	Al Qaeda		U.S. born			
2006	22	Al Qaeda		U.S. born			
2006	31	Al Qaeda		U.S. born			
2006	27	Al Qaeda		Visa unk			
2006	22		Convert	U.S. born	HSG	INC	
2007	22	Al Qaeda	Born	NAT	Some uni	INC	
2007	23	Al Qaeda	Born	LPR	HSG	INC	
2007	24	Al Qaeda	Born	LPR	<HS	REL	
2007	28	Al Qaeda	Born	Illegal	<HS	INC	
2007	26	Al Qaeda	Born	Illegal	<HS	INC	
2007	23	Al Qaeda	Born	Illegal	<HS	INC	
2007	63	Al Qaeda	Convert	NAT		INC	

Plot or Attack (attacks are highlighted)	Name	Gender	Year Born	Country of Origin	Year Entered the United States (if foreign born)	Age at Entry into the United States (if foreign born)	Years in the United States Before Arrest, Attack, or Death (if foreign born)
Plot to bomb fuel pipelines at JFK International Airport	Abdul Kadir	Male	1952	Guyana			
Plot to bomb fuel pipelines at JFK International Airport	Kareem Ibrahim	Male	1946	Trinidad			
Plot to bomb fuel pipelines at JFK International Airport	Abdel Nur	Male	1950	Guyana			
Plots against various targets	Christopher Paul	Male	1964	United States			
Plot to blow up the Long Island Rail Road	Bryant Neal Vinas	Male	1982	United States			
Plots to blow up synagogues and shoot down military planes	James Cromitie	Male	1964	United States			
Plots to blow up synagogues and shoot down military planes	David Williams	Male	1981	United States			
Plots to blow up synagogues and shoot down military planes	Onta Williams	Male	1976	United States			
Plots to blow up synagogues and shoot down military planes	Laguerre Payen	Male	1981	Haiti			
Shooting attack against a Little Rock recruiting office	Carlos Bledsoe	Male	1985	United States			
Raleigh jihad group plot against Marine Corps Base Quantico	Daniel Patrick Boyd	Male	1970	United States			
Raleigh jihad group plot against Marine Corps Base Quantico	Zakariya Boyd	Male	1989	United States			
Raleigh jihad group plot against Marine Corps Base Quantico	Dylan Boyd	Male	1987	United States			

Year of Plot or Attack	Age at Arrest or Attack	Name of Associated Group (if any)	Converted or Born into Islam	Residency	Education	Status	Note
2007	55	Al Qaeda	Convert	Guyana	BA/BS	INC	Never came to the United States
2007	61	Al Qaeda, Jamaat Al Muslimeen	Born	Trinidad		INC	Never came to the United States
2007	57	Al Qaeda	Born	Guyana		INC	Never came to the United States
2007	43	Al Qaeda	Convert	U.S. born	BA/BS	INC	
2008	26	Al Qaeda, Taliban	Convert	U.S. born	Some uni	INC	
2009	44	JEM	Convert	U.S. born		INC	
2009	28	JEM	Convert	U.S. born		INC	
2009	32	JEM	Convert	U.S. born		INC	
2009	27	JEM	Convert	LPR		INC	
2009	23	Al Qaeda in the Arabian Peninsula	Convert	U.S. born	Some uni	INC	
2009	39	Hezb-e-Islami Gulbuddin	Convert	U.S. born	HSG	INC	
2009	20		Convert	U.S. born	Some uni		
2009	22		Convert	U.S. born	Some uni		

Plot or Attack (attacks are highlighted)	Name	Gender	Year Born	Country of Origin	Year Entered the United States (if foreign born)	Age at Entry into the United States (if foreign born)	Years in the United States Before Arrest, Attack, or Death (if foreign born)
Raleigh jihad group plot against Marine Corps Base Quantico	Mohammad Hassan	Male	1987	United States			
Raleigh jihad group plot against Marine Corps Base Quantico	Jude Mohammad	Male	1988	United States			
Raleigh jihad group plot against Marine Corps Base Quantico	Anes Subasic	Male	1976	Bosnia			
Raleigh jihad group plot against Marine Corps Base Quantico	Ziyad Yaghi	Male	1988	Jordan	1990	2	19
Raleigh jihad group plot against Marine Corps Base Quantico	Hysen Sherifi	Male	1985	Kosovo	1999	14	10
Plot to suicide-bomb the New York City subway	Najibullah Zazi	Male	1985	Afghanistan	1999	14	10
Plot to suicide-bomb the New York City subway	Adis Medunjanin	Male	1984	Bosnia	1994	10	15
Plot to suicide-bomb the New York City subway	Ahmad Afzali	Male	1972	Afghanistan	1979	7	30
Plot to suicide-bomb the New York City subway	Zarein Ahmedzay	Male	1985	Afghanistan			
Plot to suicide-bomb the New York City subway	Mohammed Wali Zazi	Male	1955	Afghanistan	1990	35	18
Plot to suicide-bomb the New York City subway	Amanullah Zazi	Male	1987	Afghanistan	2009	22	0
Plot to use planes to attack a building in Dallas	Hosam Smadi	Male	1990	Jordan	2007	17	2
Plot to blow up a federal courthouse in Springfield, Illinois	Michael Finton	Male	1980	United States			

Year of Plot or Attack	Age at Arrest or Attack	Name of Associated Group (if any)	Converted or Born into Islam	Residency	Education	Status	Note
2009	22		Born	U.S. born	BA/BS	INC	
2009	20	Al Qaeda, Pakistani Taliban	Born	U.S. born	Some uni	DEC	
2009	33		Born	NAT		INC	
2009	21		Convert	NAT	<HS	INC	
2009	24		Born	LPR	Some uni	INC	
2009	24	Al Qaeda	Born	LPR	<HS		
2009	25	Al Qaeda	Born	NAT	BA/BS	INC	
2009	37	Al Qaeda	Born	LPR	HSG		
2009	24	Al Qaeda	Born	NAT	Some uni		
2009	53	Al Qaeda	Born	NAT	<HS		
2009	22	Al Qaeda	Born	IR-2 visa			
2009	19	Al Qaeda	Born	B-2 visa	<HS	INC	
2009	29	Al Qaeda	Convert	U.S. born	HSG	INC	

Plot or Attack (attacks are highlighted)	Name	Gender	Year Born	Country of Origin	Year Entered the United States (if foreign born)	Age at Entry into the United States (if foreign born)	Years in the United States Before Arrest, Attack, or Death (if foreign born)
Shooting plot against U.S. shopping and diplomatic targets	Tarek Mehanna	Male	1982	United States			
Shooting plot against U.S. shopping and diplomatic targets	Ahmad Abousamra	Male	1981	France			
Shooting attack at Fort Hood	Nidal Hasan	Male	1970	United States			
Plot to bomb a U.S. stadium	Raja Khan	Male	1954	Pakistan	1975	21	35
Plot to bomb the New York Stock Exchange	Khalid Ouazzani	Male	1977	Morocco	1999	22	11
Plot to bomb the New York Stock Exchange	Sabirhan Hasanoff	Male	1976	China	1993	17	17
Plot to bomb the New York Stock Exchange	Wesam El-Hanafi	Male	1976	United States			
Car-bomb attack at Times Square	Faisal Shahzad	Male	1979	Pakistan	1999	20	11
Plot to assassinate various targets	Paul Rockwood, Jr.	Male	1975	United States			
Plot to assassinate various targets	Nadia Rockwood	Female	1974	United Kingdom			
Plot to bomb the D.C. metro near the Pentagon	Farooque Ahmed	Male	1976	Pakistan	1993	17	17
Plot to car-bomb a tree-lighting ceremony in Portland, Oregon	Mohamed Osman Mohamud	Male	1991	Somalia	1995	4	15
Plot to car-bomb a Baltimore recruiting center	Antonio Martinez	Male	1989	Nicaragua			
Plot to solicit jihadists online to kill Americans	Emerson Begolly	Male	1990	United States			

Year of Plot or Attack	Age at Arrest or Attack	Name of Associated Group (if any)	Converted or Born into Islam	Residency	Education	Status	Note
2009	27	Al Qaeda	Born	U.S. born	BA/BS	INC	
2009	28		Born	NAT	BA/BS	DEC	
2009	39	Taliban (later ISIS)	Born	U.S. born	POST	INC	
2010	56	Al Qaeda	Born	NAT		INC	
2010	33	Al Qaeda	Born	NAT		INC	
2010	34	Al Qaeda	Born	NAT	BA/BS	INC	
2010	34	Al Qaeda	Born	U.S. born	BA/BS	INC	
2010	30	Tehrik-e-Taliban	Born	NAT	POST	INC	
2010	35		Convert	U.S. born			
2010	36		Convert	NAT		REL	
2010	34	Al Qaeda	Born	NAT	POST	INC	
2010	19	Al Qaeda in the Arabian Peninsula	Born	NAT	Some uni	INC	
2010	21		Convert	NAT	<HS	INC	
2011	21		Convert	U.S. born	Some uni	INC	

Plot or Attack (attacks are highlighted)	Name	Gender	Year Born	Country of Origin	Year Entered the United States (if foreign born)	Age at Entry into the United States (if foreign born)	Years in the United States Before Arrest, Attack, or Death (if foreign born)
Plots to blow up dams, nuclear plants, or the Dallas home of former President George W. Bush	Khalid Aldawsari	Male	1991	Saudi Arabia	2008	17	3
Plot against a New York City synagogue	Ahmed Ferhani	Male	1985	Algeria	1995	10	16
Plot against a New York City synagogue	Mohamed Mamdouh	Male	1991	Morocco	1999	8	12
Shooting attacks at the Pentagon and other military facilities	Yonathan Melaku	Male	1989	Ethiopia	2005	16	6
Plot to attack Seattle military processing center	Abu Abdul-Latif	Male	1978	United States			
Plot to attack Seattle military processing center	Walli Mujahidh	Male	1979	United States			
Plot to kill President Barack Obama	Ulugbek Kodirov	Male	1990	Uzbekistan	2009	19	2
Plot to bomb restaurant near Fort Hood	Naser Jason Abdo	Male	1980	United States			
Plot to use explosives-packed model aircraft against the Pentagon and U.S. Capitol	Rezwan Ferdaus	Male	1985	United States			
Plot to pipe-bomb returning service members	José Pimentel	Male	1984	Dominican Republic	1989	5	22
Plot to bomb and seize various Tampa targets	Sami Osmakac	Male	1987	Kosovo	2000	13	12
Plot to suicide-bomb the U.S. Capitol	Amine El Khalifi	Male	1983	Morocco	1999	16	13
Plot to blow up the Federal Reserve building in New York	Quazi Nafis	Male	1991	Bangladesh	2012	21	0

Year of Plot or Attack	Age at Arrest or Attack	Name of Associated Group (if any)	Converted or Born into Islam	Residency	Education	Status	Note
2011	20		Born	Student visa	Some uni	INC	
2011	26		Born	LPR		INC	
2011	20		Born	NAT	HSG	INC	
2011	22		Convert	NAT	HSG	INC	
2011	33		Convert	U.S. born	HSG	INC	
2011	32		Convert	U.S. born		INC	
2011	21	Islamic Movement of Uzbekistan	Born	Student visa	BA/BS	INC	
2011	21		Convert	U.S. born	HSG	INC	
2011	26	Al Qaeda	Born	U.S. born	BA/BS	INC	
2011	27	Al Qaeda	Convert	NAT	Some uni	INC	
2012	25	Al Qaeda	Born	NAT	HSG	INC	
2012	29	Al Qaeda	Born	Visitor visa		INC	
2012	21	Al Qaeda	Born	Student visa		INC	

Plot or Attack (attacks are highlighted)	Name	Gender	Year Born	Country of Origin	Year Entered the United States (if foreign born)	Age at Entry into the United States (if foreign born)	Years in the United States Before Arrest, Attack, or Death (if foreign born)
Plot to blow up various New York sites	Sheheryar Qazi	Male	1982	Pakistan	2000	18	12
Plot to blow up various New York sites	Raees Alam Qazi	Male	1992	Pakistan	2000	8	12
Plot to rob various targets leaving no survivors	Erwin Antonio Rios	Male	1994	United States			
Plot to car-bomb an Oakland, California, bank	Matthew Aaron Llaneza	Male	1985	United States			
Pressure-cooker bomb attack at the Boston Marathon	Tamerlan Tsarnaev	Male	1986	Russia	2003	16	10
Pressure-cooker bomb attack at the Boston Marathon	Dzhokhar Tsarnaev	Male	1993	Kyrgyzstan	2002	9	10
Plot supporting the Islamic Movement of Uzbekistan	Fazliddin Kurbanov	Male	1983	Uzbekistan	2009	26	4
Plot to car-bomb the Wichita Dwight D. Eisenhower National Airport	Terry Lee Loewen	Male	1955	United States			
Shooting attacks on Washington State and New Jersey targets	Ali Muhammad Brown	Male	1985	United States			
Beheading attacks at Oklahoma City food-processing plant	Alton Nolen	Male	1984	United States			
Plot to shoot U.S. service members	Mufid Elfgeeh	Male	1984	Yemen	1997	13	17
Hatchet attacks on New York City police officers	Zale Thompson	Male	1982	United States			
Plot to bomb the U.S. Capitol and assassinate the President	Christopher Cornell	Male	1994	United States			

Year of Plot or Attack	Age at Arrest or Attack	Name of Associated Group (if any)	Converted or Born into Islam	Residency	Education	Status	Note
2012	30	Al Qaeda in the Arabian Peninsula	Born	NAT	HSG	INC	
2012	20	Al Qaeda in the Arabian Peninsula	Born	NAT	HSG	INC	
2013	19		Convert	U.S. born	<HS or HSG	INC	
2013	28		Convert	U.S. born		INC	
2013	26		Born	Asylum	Some uni	KILL	
2013	19		Born	NAT	Some uni	INC	
2013	30	Islamic Movement of Uzbekistan	Born	Refugee		INC	
2013	58	Al Qaeda in the Arabian Peninsula	Convert	U.S. born			
2014	29	ISIS	Convert	U.S. born		INC	
2014	30		Convert	U.S. born		INC	
2014	30	ISIS	Born	NAT		INC	
2014	32		Convert	U.S. born	Some uni	KILL	
2015	20	ISIS	Convert	U.S. born	HSG	INC	

Plot or Attack (attacks are highlighted)	Name	Gender	Year Born	Country of Origin	Year Entered the United States (if foreign born)	Age at Entry into the United States (if foreign born)	Years in the United States Before Arrest, Attack, or Death (if foreign born)
Plot to sniper-attack targets using bullets marked "ISIS"	Miguel Moran Diaz	Male	1970	Cuba	1989	19	26
Plot to kill soldiers at North Carolina military base	Zakaryia Abdin	Male	1999	United States			
Plot to attack a Joliet, Illinois, armory	Jonas Edmonds	Male	1986	United States			
Plot to attack a Joliet, Illinois, armory	Hasan Edmonds	Male	1993	United States			
Plot to bomb various U.S. targets	Asia Siddiqui	Female	1984	Saudi Arabia			
Plot to bomb various U.S. targets	Noelle Velentzas	Female	1987	United States			
Tweeted threats against Justice Department officials	Mahamed Abukar Said	Male	1995	Ethiopia	1996	1	19
Plot to suicide-bomb Fort Riley, Kansas	John T. Booker, Jr.	Male	1995	United States			
Plot to suicide-bomb Fort Riley, Kansas	Alexander Blair	Male	1987	United States			
Plot to attack a police station and kill military service members	Munir Abdulkader	Male	1995	Eritrea			
Shooting attack at a Garland, Texas, museum featuring cartoons of Muhammad	Elton Simpson	Male	1985	United States			
Shooting attack at a Garland, Texas, museum featuring cartoons of Muhammad	Nadir Soofi	Male	1981	United States			

Year of Plot or Attack	Age at Arrest or Attack	Name of Associated Group (if any)	Converted or Born into Islam	Residency	Education	Status	Note
2015	45	ISIS	Convert	?		INC	
2015	16	ISIS	Born	U.S. born	<HS	INC	
2015	29	ISIS	Convert	U.S. born		INC	
2015	22	ISIS	Convert	U.S. born	HSG	INC	
2015	31	ISIS, al Qaeda in the Arabian Peninsula	Born	NAT	BA/BS	INC	
2015	28	ISIS, al Qaeda in the Arabian Peninsula	Convert	U.S. born	POST	INC	
2015	20	ISIS	Born	?	Some uni	REL	
2015	20	ISIS	Convert	U.S. born	HSG	INC	
2015	28	ISIS	Convert	U.S. born		INC	
2015	21	ISIS	Born	NAT	Some uni	INC	
2015	30	Al Shabaab, ISIS	Convert	U.S. born	Some uni	KILL	
2015	34	ISIS	Born	U.S. born	Some uni	KILL	

Plot or Attack (attacks are highlighted)	Name	Gender	Year Born	Country of Origin	Year Entered the United States (if foreign born)	Age at Entry into the United States (if foreign born)	Years in the United States Before Arrest, Attack, or Death (if foreign born)
Shooting attack at a Garland, Texas, museum featuring cartoons of Muhammad	Abdul Kareem	Male	1972	United States			
Plot to behead a police officer	David Wright	Male	1989	United States			
Plot to behead a police officer	Usaamah Rahim	Male	1989	United States			
Plot to behead a police officer	Nicholas Rovinski	Male	1991	United States			
Mass-shooting plot against people in Virginia and North Carolina	Justin Sullivan	Male	1996	United States			
Plot to make and use a pressure-cooker bomb against New York City targets	Munther Omar Saleh	Male	1995	United States			
Plot to make and use a pressure-cooker bomb against New York City targets	Fareed Mumuni	Male	1994	Ghana			
Plot to make and use a pressure-cooker bomb against New York City targets	Imran Rabbani	Male	1998	United States			
Plot to bomb Florida targets on behalf of ISIS	Harlem Suarez	Male	1992	Cuba	2004	12	11
Shooting attacks at a Chattanooga recruiting office and Navy Operational Support Center	Muhammad Youssef Abdulazeez	Male	1990	Kuwait	1990	0	24
Plot to bomb a university and broadcast executions of students	Alexander Ciccolo	Male	1992	United States			
Plots to attack uniformed personnel	Abdirahman Sheik Mohamud	Male	1992	Somalia	1994	2	21
Plot to assassinate the pope and bomb the surrounding area	Santos Colon, Jr.	Male	2000	?			

Year of Plot or Attack	Age at Arrest or Attack	Name of Associated Group (if any)	Converted or Born into Islam	Residency	Education	Status	Note
2015	43	ISIS	Convert	U.S. born		INC	
2015	25	ISIS	Convert	U.S. born	Some uni	INC	
2015	26	ISIS	Born	U.S. born	Some uni	KILL	
2015	24	ISIS	Convert	U.S. born	HSG	INC	
2015	19	ISIS	Convert	U.S. born		INC	
2015	20	ISIS	Born	U.S. born	Some uni	INC	
2015	21	ISIS	Born	NAT	Some uni	INC	
2015	17	ISIS	Born	U.S. born	HSG	INC	
2015	23	ISIS	Convert	LPR	<HS	INC	
2015	24		Born	NAT	BA/BS	KILL	
2015	23	ISIS	Convert	U.S. born		INC	
2015	23	Jabhat al-Nusra	Born	NAT	HSG	INC	
2015	15	ISIS	Convert	U.S. citizen		INC	

Plot or Attack (attacks are highlighted)	Name	Gender	Year Born	Country of Origin	Year Entered the United States (if foreign born)	Age at Entry into the United States (if foreign born)	Years in the United States Before Arrest, Attack, or Death (if foreign born)
Stabbing attacks at the University of California Merced	Faisal Mohammad	Male	1997	United States			
Explicit calling for the killings of specific service personnel	Terrence McNeil	Male	1990	United States			
Shooting attack on the Inland Regional Center in San Bernardino, California	Syed Farook	Male	1987	United States			
Shooting attack on the Inland Regional Center in San Bernardino, California	Tashfeen Malik	Female	1986	Pakistan	2014	28	1
Shooting attack on the Inland Regional Center in San Bernardino, California	Enrique Marquez, Jr.	Male	1991	United States			
Plot to shoot people at the Garland, Texas, exhibit of cartoons of Muhammad	Mohamed Abdullahi Hassan	Male	1990	Somalia			
Receipt of funds from ISIS to plan an attack	Mohamed Yousef Elshinawy	Male	1985	Egypt			
Plot to attack Rochester restaurant diners with machetes	Emanuel Lutchman	Male	1990	United States			
Plot to bomb a Houston shopping mall	Omar Faraj Saeed al Hardan	Male	1991	Iraq	2009	18	7
Plot a mass shooting at a Masonic temple in Milwaukee	Samy Mohamed Hamzeh	Male	1992	United States			
Shooting attack on a Philadelphia police officer	Edward Archer	Male	1986	United States			

Year of Plot or Attack	Age at Arrest or Attack	Name of Associated Group (if any)	Converted or Born into Islam	Residency	Education	Status	Note
2015	18		Born	U.S. born	Some uni	KILL	
2015	25	ISIS	Convert	U.S. born		INC	
2015	28	ISIS	Born	U.S. born	POST	KILL	
2015	29	ISIS	Born	LPR	BA/BS	KILL	
2015	24		Convert	U.S. born	Some uni	INC	
2015	25	Al Shabaab	Born	LPR	HSG	INC	In prison in Somalia
2015	30	ISIS	Born	NAT		INC	
2015	25	ISIS	Convert	U.S. born	<HS	INC	
2016	24	ISIS	Born	LPR		INC	
2016	23		Born	U.S. born	Some uni	INC	
2016	30	ISIS	Convert	U.S. born	Some uni	INC	

Plot or Attack (attacks are highlighted)	Name	Gender	Year Born	Country of Origin	Year Entered the United States (if foreign born)	Age at Entry into the United States (if foreign born)	Years in the United States Before Arrest, Attack, or Death (if foreign born)
Recruiting trainees for attacks against unknown targets on behalf of ISIS	Erick Jamal Hendricks	Male	1981	United States			
Plot to shoot at a Detroit church and skin his victims	Khalil Abu Rayyan	Male	1994	United States			
Plot to bomb a Florida synagogue	James Gonzalo Medina	Male	1976	United States			
Plot to kill the President	Alex Hernandez	Male	1985	United States			
Mass-shooting attack at the Pulse nightclub in Orlando	Omar Mateen	Male	1986	United States			
Plot to use grenades against unknown targets	Sebastian Gregerson	Male	1987	United States			
Plot to bomb various government offices in Tucson and Mesa	Mahin Khan	Male	1998	United States			
Mass-shooting plot against military personnel	Mohamed Bailor Jalloh	Male	1989	Sierra Leone			
Stabbing attacks at a St. Cloud, Minnesota, shopping mall	Dahir Adan	Male	1996	Somalia	1996	0	20
Pipe-bomb and pressure-cooker bomb attacks in New Jersey and New York	Ahmad Khan Rahami	Male	1988	Afghanistan	1995	7	21
Plot to kill an ISIS-specified U.S. service member	Nelash Mohamed Das	Male	1992	Bangladesh	1995	3	21
Plot to bomb an Arizona prison	Thomas Orville Bastian	Male	1977	United States			
Plot to bomb an Arizona prison	Michelle Bastian	Female	1967	United States			

Year of Plot or Attack	Age at Arrest or Attack	Name of Associated Group (if any)	Converted or Born into Islam	Residency	Education	Status	Note
2016	35	ISIS	Convert	U.S. born	HSG	INC	
2016	21	ISIS	Born	U.S. born		INC	
2016	40	ISIS	Convert	U.S. born		INC	
2016	31		Convert	U.S. born		INC	
2016	29	ISIS	Born	U.S. born	Some uni	KILL	
2016	29		Convert	U.S. born	Some uni	INC	
2016	18	ISIS	Born	U.S. born	<HS	INC	
2016	26	ISIS	Born	NAT		INC	
2016	20		Born	NAT		KILL	
2016	28		Born	NAT	Some uni	INC	
2016	24	ISIS	Born	LPR		INC	
2016	39		Convert	U.S. born		INC	
2016	49			U.S. born		INC	

Plot or Attack (attacks are highlighted)	Name	Gender	Year Born	Country of Origin	Year Entered the United States (if foreign born)	Age at Entry into the United States (if foreign born)	Years in the United States Before Arrest, Attack, or Death (if foreign born)
Car-ramming and stabbing attacks at Ohio State University	Abdul Razak Ali Artan	Male	1998	Somalia	2014	16	2
Shooting attack on a Denver police officer	Joshua Cummings	Male	1980	United States			
Plot to bomb transit targets in Kansas City, Missouri	Robert Hester	Male	1992	United States			

Year of Plot or Attack	Age at Arrest or Attack	Name of Associated Group (if any)	Converted or Born into Islam	Residency	Education	Status	Note
2016	18		Born	LPR	Some uni	KILL	
2017	37		Convert	U.S. born		INC	
2017	25	ISIS	Convert	U.S. born		INC	

Epilogue

Subsequent to our completing the research for this report, three more incidents occurred. On June 21, 2017, Amor M. Ftouhi, a 49-year-old man with dual Tunisian and Canadian citizenship, stabbed a police officer at the airport in Flint, Michigan. At the moment of the attack, he shouted, "Allahu Akbar" (God is greater), a common jihadist battle cry, and, "You have killed people in Syria, Iraq, and Afghanistan, and we are all going to die," causing the incident to be viewed as a terrorist attack, although the U.S. terrorist statute has not been invoked as of this writing. Ftouhi, who is married and has three children, was unknown to Canadian and U.S. authorities and is believed to have acted alone. He had entered the country five days before the attack, probably intending to carry out the attack.

On October 20, 2017, Vicente Adolfo Solano, a 53-year-old convert to Islam, activated the timer of what he believed was a bomb but in fact was an inert device that FBI agents posing as members of ISIS had provided to him. His intended target was the crowded food court of a Miami shopping mall. Solano, who is a citizen of Honduras, arrived in the United States sometime in the late 1990s and has remained in the country on temporary protected status. The addition of this case would bring the total number of jihadist terrorist plots to 87.

Finally, on October 31, 2017, Sayfullo Saipov, a 29-year-old legal permanent resident from Uzbekistan, deliberately drove a rented truck onto a bike path in Lower Manhattan to run over cyclists and pedestrians, eventually crashing into a school bus. Eight people died, and 11 people were injured in the attack. Upon crashing into the school bus, Saipov exited his car, shouting, "Allahu Akbar" and waving what were initially reported to be two pistols (but in fact were a pellet gun and a paintball gun). Police shot and wounded him. A note was found at the scene pledging allegiance to ISIS, and, after his arrest, Saipov reportedly indicated that he was proud of his attack. Saipov had entered the United States in 2010. He was married and had three children.

The addition of these cases would bring the total number of jihadist attacks planned in the United States to 21, resulting in a total of 103 deaths, the total number of attackers to 26, and the total number of plotters and attackers to 180. Ftouhi's attack would fall into the separate category of foreign-based terrorist attempts, like those of Richard Reid and Umar Abdulmutallab.

About the Author

Brian Michael Jenkins is a senior adviser to the president of the RAND Corporation and author of numerous books, reports, and articles on terrorism-related topics, including *Will Terrorists Go Nuclear?* (2008, Prometheus Books). He formerly served as chair of the Political Science Department at RAND. On the occasion of the ten-year anniversary of 9/11, Jenkins initiated a RAND effort to take stock of America's policy reactions and give thoughtful consideration to future strategy. That effort is presented in *The Long Shadow of 9/11: America's Response to Terrorism* (Brian Michael Jenkins and John Paul Godges, eds., 2011).

Commissioned in the infantry, Jenkins became a paratrooper and a captain in the Green Berets. He is a decorated combat veteran, having served in the Seventh Special Forces Group in the Dominican Republic and with the Fifth Special Forces Group in Vietnam. He returned to Vietnam as a member of the Long Range Planning Task Group and received the Department of the Army's highest award for his service.

In 1996, President Bill Clinton appointed Jenkins to the White House Commission on Aviation Safety and Security. From 1999 to 2000, he served as adviser to the National Commission on Terrorism and, in 2000, was appointed to the U.S. Comptroller General's advisory board. He is a research associate at the Mineta Transportation Institute, where he directs the continuing research on protecting surface transportation against terrorist attacks. Jenkins is the author of more than 150 reports, articles, and testimonies, including the following:

Brian Michael Jenkins, *A Saudi-Led Military Alliance to Fight Terrorism: Welcome Muscle in the Fight Against Terrorism, Desert Mirage, or Bad Idea?*, RAND Corporation, PE-189-RC, 2016. As of October 31, 2017: https://www.rand.org/pubs/perspectives/PE189.html

Amichay Ayalon and Brian Michael Jenkins, *War by What Means, According to Whose Rules? The Challenge for Democracies Facing Asymmetric Conflicts: Proceedings of a RAND–Israel Democracy Institute Workshop, December 3–4, 2014*, RAND Corporation, CF-334-CMEPP, 2015. As of October 31, 2017: https://www.rand.org/pubs/conf_proceedings/CF334.html

Brian Michael Jenkins, *When Jihadis Come Marching Home: The Terrorist Threat Posed by Westerners Returning from Syria and Iraq*, RAND Corporation, PE-130-1-RC, 2014. As of October 31, 2017: https://www.rand.org/pubs/perspectives/PE130-1.html

Brian Michael Jenkins, *When Armies Divide: The Security of Nuclear Arsenals During Revolts, Coups, and Civil Wars*, 2013.

Brian Michael Jenkins, *Al Qaeda in Its Third Decade: Irreversible Decline or Imminent Victory?* RAND Corporation, OP-362-RC, 2012. As of October 31, 2017: https://www.rand.org/pubs/occasional_papers/OP362.html

Brian Michael Jenkins, *Stray Dogs and Virtual Armies: Radicalization and Recruitment to Jihadist Terrorism in the United States Since 9/11*, RAND Corporation, OP-343-RC, 2011. As of October 31, 2017: https://www.rand.org/pubs/occasional_papers/OP343.html

Brian Michael Jenkins and John P. Godges, eds., *The Long Shadow of 9/11: America's Response to Terrorism*, RAND Corporation, MG-1107-RC, 2011. As of October 31, 2017: https://www.rand.org/pubs/monographs/MG1107.html

Brian Michael Jenkins, *Unconquerable Nation: Knowing Our Enemy, Strengthening Ourselves*, RAND Corporation, MG-454-RC, 2006. As of October 31, 2017: https://www.rand.org/pubs/monographs/MG454.html

Paul Wilkinson and Brian Michael Jenkins, eds., *Aviation Terrorism and Security*, London: Routledge, 2007.

Brian Michael Jenkins, "The Jihadists' Operational Code," in David Aaron, ed., *Three Years After: Next Steps in the War on Terror*, RAND Corporation, CF-212-RC, 2005, pp. 3–8. As of October 31, 2017: https://www.rand.org/pubs/conf_proceedings/CF212.html

Brian Michael Jenkins, *Countering al Qaeda: An Appreciation of the Situation and Suggestions for Strategy*, RAND Corporation, MR-1620-RC, 2002. As of October 31, 2017: https://www.rand.org/pubs/monograph_reports/MR1620.html

Paul K. Davis and Brian Michael Jenkins, *Deterrence and Influence in Counterterrorism: A Component in the War on al Qaeda*, RAND Corporation, MR-1619-DARPA, 2002. As of October 31, 2017: https://www.rand.org/pubs/monograph_reports/MR1619.html

Acknowledgments

I am grateful to many. I would like to thank Michael Rich, president and chief executive officer of the RAND Corporation, for continuing corporate support of my independent research.

Although her name does not appear on the cover, I want to acknowledge the significant contribution made by Anita Szafran in this effort. She constructed the spreadsheets and provided vital research assistance in digging for the details that one would have imagined were readily available but proved remarkable difficult to track down. She responded diligently (and gracefully) to my relentless interrogations and made endless revisions, adding sound judgments, as we developed the final conclusions. She is a treasure to RAND's Knowledge Services. I benefited greatly from our partnership.

I would also like to thank Andriy Bega, Roberta Shanman, and Sachi Yagyu for their assistance. It was anticipated that this report would provoke controversy, which required that every assertion be closely examined and thoroughly supported. Patrick B. Johnston and Heather J. Williams provided detailed reviews that were of great assistance. Several other people provided additional information, helpful reviews, and thoughtful comments. I would like to specifically thank Richard Daddario, Karen Greenberg, Katrina Griffin-Moore, Seth Jones, and David A. Lubarsky. And finally, I am grateful to Janet DeLand, whose always-skillful editing clarifies my writing, and to Lisa Bernard for the final editorial review.

Abbreviations

CVE	countering violent extremism
DHS	U.S. Department of Homeland Security
FBI	Federal Bureau of Investigation
ISIS	Islamic State of Iraq and Syria
JFK	John F. Kennedy
PATH	Port Authority Trans-Hudson
UK	United Kingdom

RAND Ventures

The RAND Corporation is a research organization that develops solutions to public policy challenges to help make communities throughout the world safer and more secure, healthier and more prosperous. RAND is nonprofit, nonpartisan, and committed to the public interest.

RAND Ventures is a vehicle for investing in policy solutions. Philanthropic contributions support our ability to take the long view, tackle tough and often-controversial topics, and share our findings in innovative and compelling ways. RAND's research findings and recommendations are based on data and evidence, and therefore do not necessarily reflect the policy preferences or interests of its clients, donors, or supporters.

Funding for this venture was provided by gifts from RAND supporters and income from operations.